AL TOUBY
HURST
EMI UNDER GLASS

HEMI UNDER GLASS

Bob Riggle and his Wheel-Standing Mopars

CarTech®

Mark Fletcher &
Richard Truesdell

EMI UNDER GLASS
A ROLLING RESEARCH LABOATORY

CarTech®

CarTech®, Inc.
838 Lake Street South
Forest Lake, MN 55025
Phone: 651-277-1200 or 800-551-4754
Fax: 651-277-1203
www.cartechbooks.com

Edit by Wes Eisenschenk
Layout by Connie DeFlorin

ISBN 978-1-61325-561-2
Item No. CT670

Library of Congress Cataloging-in-Publication Data

Names: Truesdell, Richard, author. | Fletcher, Mark, 1959- author.
Title: Hemi Under Glass : Bob Riggle and his wheel-standing Mopars / Rich Truesdell and Mark Fletcher.
Description: Forest Lake, MN : CarTech, Inc., [2021] | "Item No. CT670."
Identifiers: LCCN 2021058711 | ISBN 9781613255612 (paperback)
Subjects: LCSH: Dragsters--United States--History. | Dodge automobile--History. | Hurst Performance--History. | Riggle, Bob, 1935- | Drag racers--United States--Biography. | Automobile mechanics--United States--Biography.
Classification: LCC TL236.2 .T78 2021 | DDC 629.228/5--dc23
LC record available at https://lccn.loc.gov/2021058711

Written, edited, and designed in the U.S.A.
Printed in China
10 9 8 7 6 5 4 3 2 1

PUBLISHER'S NOTE: In reporting history, the images required to tell the tale will vary greatly in quality, especially by modern photographic standards. While some images in this volume are not up to those digital standards, we have included them, as we feel they are an important element in telling the story.

DISTRIBUTION BY:

Europe
PGUK
63 Hatton Garden
London EC1N 8LE, England
Phone: 020 7061 1980 • Fax: 020 7242 3725
www.pguk.co.uk

Australia
Renniks Publications Ltd.
3/37-39 Green Street
Banksmeadow, NSW 2109, Australia
Phone: 2 9695 7055 • Fax: 2 9695 7355
www.renniks.com

Canada
Login Canada
300 Saulteaux Crescent
Winnipeg, MB, R3J 3T2 Canada
Phone: 800 665 1148 • Fax: 800 665 0103
www.lb.ca

Table of Contents

Acknowledgments

This book would not be possible without the assistance of its subject: the remarkable Bob Riggle. When Bob began taking photographs almost seven decades ago, he probably never could have imagined the story that they would tell and document.

At a very young age, Bob's daredevil approach to life led to many memorable events during a professional career that ultimately spanned the better part of seven decades. It's a career that his many friends still reminisce about today.

Over his lifetime, Bob has been helped along the way by many people. However, Bob will freely admit that no one has been more important than his wife of more than 60 years, Nanci. Over the course of their marriage, they have been true partners on and off the track.

Bob's career received a huge boost when he joined the team at Hurst Performance in Warminster, Pennsylvania. Many of those coworkers helped by collaborating for this book. Some of them are known personalities, and the reader will recognize them. They include Hurst Performance founders George Hurst and Bill Campbell, who recently passed away. Others include Linda Vaughn, Jack "Doc" Watson, and Shirley Shahan (Bridges), each of whom contributed during Bob Riggle's long and storied career.

Other names may be less known but were still highly influential. Former Hurst employees, such as Dave Landrith, Don Morton, Bill McDonnell, Steve Weiner, and Marty Danko, contributed to this book along with many Hurst collectors, such as Joe Spagnoli, Bill Sefton, and Pete Serio.

This book is dedicated to the courageous men and women of drag racing who shared their talents with the general public in an up-close-and-personal way. In the 1960s, as drag racing was emerging as a popular spectator sport, many participants became local and national favorites and were well-known names. Many of these racing careers were a short portion of their (and our) lives. After their racing careers ended, most of Bob's colleagues lived more traditional lives, becoming our neighbors, coworkers, and friends.

We both consider it the honor of a lifetime to share with you Bob Riggle's unique story. Throughout his long career with the related fame and accolades, Bob Riggle remained personable and approachable. More than anything, it's been his joy to interact with his many fans, right up to his last time behind the wheel. We hope that this book will create many additional opportunities for Bob Riggle to interact with his fans for years to come.

To that end, we both are proud to be a small part in helping to tell his story.

— Mark Fletcher and Richard Truesdell

Foreword by Linda Vaughn

When asked to write the foreword for *Hemi Under Glass*, knowing that it was Bob's biography, I said that it would be an honor. After all, I've known Bob for more than five decades, and during that time, our careers have remained greatly intertwined.

I joined Hurst in 1966 after winning the title of Miss Hurst Golden Shifter. By then, Bob was already a well-established crew member. He was working on the team supporting the *Hurst Hemi Under Glass* Plymouth Barracuda, which for the 1965 season was driven by Bill Shrewsberry.

The 1966 season was when things all came together at Hurst, which cemented my lifelong friendship with Bob and his beautiful wife, Nanci. There were big changes at Hurst for the 1966 season. First, Bob moved into the driver's seat for the *Hemi Under Glass* as Bill Shrewsberry departed. Also, George Hurst made public his decision to build a second exhibition car, the *Hurst Hairy Olds*, which was powered by two Oldsmobile V-8s and driven by Joe Schubeck.

Having served 12 years in the Navy, George Hurst believed that his company should always have a close relationship with the armed forces through direct involvement with enlisted men at various bases. Over the years, Bob and I made many joint appearances at military bases around the nation. On the visits to naval bases, several times we were treated to flyovers by the Blue Angels. That was always a thrill.

In 1966 with Bob in Mexico City, Mexico, I recall one event that was supporting that year's Formula 1 race. I'm not sure that the international Formula 1 drivers knew what to make of Bob's quarter-mile trips with the front wheels off the ground, but they were certainly impressed and the crowd was certainly pleased. The other thing I remember from that weekend was that the four Monkees, from the TV show, were there performing. Looking back, I can honestly say that every event we did together was special to us as well as the participants.

Another noteworthy memory from that era was an appearance in Puerto Rico. The crowd became really excited, pushed over a fence, and surrounded us. It evolved into what I recall as the "touching incident." One of the fans touched me, and I laid him out. After that, the rest of the team surrounded me, and Bob served as my bodyguard. He made sure that I was never bothered like that ever again. He became very protective—almost like a big brother.

A consistent part of Bob's public life, touring all those years, was his wife, Nanci. She was very involved and very much a member of the Hurst team. We loved doing things together. I'm looking forward to spending time with both of them, as we'll both have books of our own to sign.

I am so pleased that with this book, Bob is now receiving the attention that he so richly deserves. He's such a modest and humble man but one who over the years has brought so much joy to so many people.

The final thing that I want to say is what a wonderful man Bob is. Knowing him for more than 50 years, I can say that he is an honorable, Christian man with wonderful values and a heart of gold. I am so proud to call him my friend. But in reality, we are more than just friends, we are a Hurst family.

Chapter 1

Bob's Early Years

Bob and his brother Dale spent their earliest years at the Oesterlen Children's Home in Springfield, Ohio. They were close to each other for the seven years they remained in the foster home.

The Great Depression began when the stock market crashed on October 29, 1929. The ripple of this disaster eventually touched the entire globe. The economic recovery was lengthy and proved to be arduous for every nation. Although the beginning date is etched into the memory of many, the ending of this downturn is much more difficult to pinpoint.

Like the end to an illness, the recovery was subtle and measured in small accomplishments rather than a single sudden occurrence. America's Midwest was slower to feel the negative effects of the stock market crash and therefore remained more stable due to the continued need for farmers to feed the American people.

Over the next 10 years, the depression slowly retreated into a recession, and life went on in the primarily agricultural Midwest. New technologies and the manufacturing industries that spawned from them helped America slowly recover during the following decade. The experiences and hardships endured during this historic period helped shape the drive and resiliency of the next generation.

Robert Riggle was born in July 1935, which was just 6 years into the Great Depression. The enduring poor economic conditions had a huge impact on the path that his life would take. His earliest memories began at just 2 years old when his brother Dale, who was 11 months older, accompanied him as they entered into the Oesterlen Children's Home in Springfield, Ohio, a state-supported foster home. Bob and Dale were placed there in 1937, when his mother could no longer afford to support 4 children by herself after her husband left for parts unknown.

Springfield is located more than 100 miles away from Bob and Dale's hometown of Mansfield. Therefore, the boys didn't see their mother

A final family photo was taken in the front yard of the family's Mansfield, Ohio, home on the day that Bob and Dale were taken to the foster home in Springfield, Ohio. Because of the 100-mile distance between the locations, family visits were infrequent in Bob's early years.

The two young Riggle boys are dwarfed on the front steps of the Oesterlen foster home. Even though Dale was only 11 months older than Bob, they were housed in separate dorm rooms and attended different classes.

or their other two siblings very often during the 7 years that they remained in the children's home.

Their mother continued to live with her family in Mansfield, which was also the location for the Ohio State reformatory that was in continual operation for more than 100 years from 1886 through 1990. This ominous prison structure was used as the movie set for *The Shawshank Redemption*, which was filmed there in 1994.

During and after the Great Depression, the largest employer in Mansfield was the growing Westinghouse Company, which manufactured large electric home appliances. As the United States continued to recover from the depressed conditions in the 1930s, Westinghouse of Mansfield built electric washing machines and refrigerators. As electrical services expanded into the rural communities, the electric appliances replaced the noisy and awkward two-stroke, gasoline-powered washing machines. Likewise, the electric refrigerator replaced the need for daily delivery of block ice for the traditional icebox.

Bob has fond memories of his seven years at the children's home with his brother. One time, Bob was outside Dale's second-story window and asked Dale to come out and play with the other kids. Dale was sick and not allowed to come out. While Dale was hanging out the window and explaining this to Bob, he fell out and broke his arm.

During the seven years at the children's home, Bob only recalled three times that his mother made the 200-mile round trip to visit her sons. There was an unusual rule at the home that involved any toys given as presents to the children. After one week of being allowed to play with them, they were taken away to be given to children who were needier than those at the home. On one of his mother's rare visits, Bob was given a wooden rocking horse for his birthday. He was allowed to play with it that night when none of the other children were around, but the following morning when Bob woke up, it was gone. A few days later, Bob saw the horse cut up and thrown in the pile of wood to be burned.

The time at the home was simply life as Bob and Dale knew it. They lived and played with their friends. Each day they walked to Lagonda Elementary School, which they attended with the other children of Springfield. Occasionally, the housemates departed—being collected by relatives or adopted by new families.

During the late 1930s when the boys were at Oesterlen, the state of Ohio juvenile support system referred to the children who were in its care as "inmates."

When Bob was 8 years old and Dale was 9, the brothers hatched a plan to run away from the home. In preparation, they stole canned goods from the pantry and stashed the extra food and supplies in the bushes outside the dorm window. They were called to the director's office and feared they had been told on by the other children or somehow their plans had been discovered. They walked into the office, convinced they were going to be punished, only be told that their mother was on the way from Mansfield to take them home permanently! Bob made sure to tell the other boys where he had hidden the pilfered supplies so that they could benefit from the aborted plan.

Bob and Dale are pictured with their mother in front of the Oesterlen Children's Home. Visits were rare, and a photograph helped Bob remember the good times when the family was able to spend time together.

his hands. When he was 10 years old, his mother asked him to fix the broken two-stroke Maytag washing machine that was kept on the back porch. He had no experience or training but quickly figured out that the two-stroke gas motor wouldn't start. He removed the spark plug and walked down to the local hardware store.

Howard, the store's owner, examined the old spark plug and sold Bob a new one along with a bottle of two-stroke oil. He explained to Bob how a two-stroke engine required a precise mixture of oil and fuel to run correctly. Bob poured out the old gas, replaced the plug, and carefully prepared the correct mixture. The machine had a kick-start similar to a motorcycle, and Bob got it running on the first kick. His mother was a bit surprised and overly appreciative of Bob's success as a mechanic. This was the catalyst for Bob's love of everything mechanical.

Return to Normalcy

It was now 1943, and Bob's mom began working for Westinghouse to support the war effort. The plant was converted from making appliances to manufacturing wing flaps for the Vought F4U Corsair fighter aircraft. Her new job was to operate a drill press, and this enabled her to purchase a large home in town where the boys were reunited with their oldest brother, Larry, and their younger sister, Beverly.

Once they returned home, the boys were enrolled in public school. Bob began third grade and soon delivered papers as a form of income. Before too long, Bob had two different newspaper routes that he completed daily on foot: a morning route and an evening route.

Over time, it became obvious to others that Bob was good with

School Years

Bob was extremely social and enjoyed his school years, but mostly he enjoyed sports and interacting with the other boys. He discovered that he had a very competitive side and played baseball and football at every opportunity.

Always the daredevil, during a sixth-grade football game, the ball was fumbled into a rather large mud

Bob was a normal teenager who filled his time with sports, cars, and work. Here he is at 16 years old playing baseball with friends in his hometown of Mansfield, Ohio.

This jalopy is the first car that Bob built. He used an old bed frame and various parts that he scrounged together to fashion an Indy-style car.

The cowl and hood were formed by bending flat sheet metal over an old steel barrel. The grille was hand-formed from raw metal.

Bob refreshed the used four-stroke Tecumseh motor and mounted it in the back with a chain drive to a single wheel. Ten cents got a local kid 10 laps around the neighborhood dirt lot.

puddle. While all the other players watched it land, Bob dove in headfirst to retrieve the ball without thinking twice about the mud.

Bob was asked to participate in the school play *Oklahoma*, where he was chosen to sing the title song in a solo. Although he was uncomfortable acting in the play, he truly enjoyed singing. Later in life, Bob sang in a band, and on many occasions, he can still be heard singing karaoke into a microphone. This vocal talent played a hand in Bob's introduction to Hurst in 1965.

When Bob was about 12 years old, he came across a Tecumseh four-stroke gas motor. Similar to the washing machine motor, it needed to be repaired. He promptly got it running and decided to build his first race car. He used a discarded steel bed frame that he cut up and bolted together to create a rigid box frame as a foundation. A salvaged Crosley steering assembly was cut down, and he mounted the motor on a platform behind the driver with an idler wheel that loosened and tightened the belt based on the movement of a pivoted clutch handle. Used sheet metal formed over a barrel acted as the front cowl and hood. He fashioned the hood and front to resemble the early 1940s Indy cars that he had seen in a magazine.

Bob was always an entrepreneur and began charging the neighborhood kids 10 cents to drive the car 10 laps around the schoolyard. Soon, the neighbor kids were lined

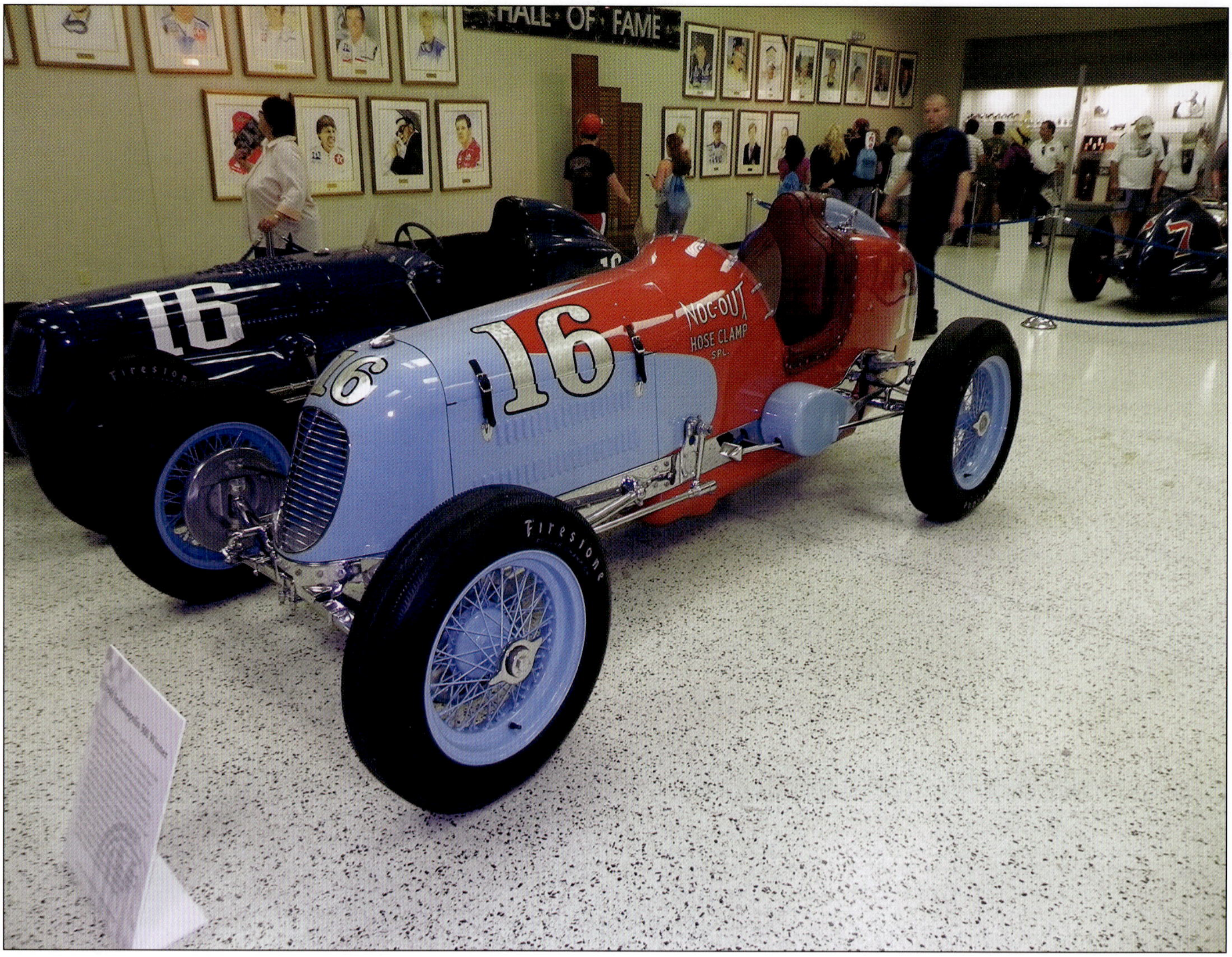

Bob fashioned his gas-powered go-kart to resemble the cars that raced and won at Indianapolis Motor Speedway, such as the car driven to victory by the team of Floyd Davis and Mauri Rose in 1941. (Photo Courtesy Keith Johnson/doctorindy.com, 2011)

up to take turns while Bob instructed them how to drive and collected the money using his coin changer from his paper routes.

A New Dad?

Bob's mom had a long-term courtship with a local grocer named Charlie, who lived in nearby Lexington, Ohio. Bob and Dale enjoyed spending time with Charlie and secretly hoped he would someday become their stepdad. Although their dream for a father was not to become a reality, Charlie had a major influence on both the boys and instilled a strong work ethic by teaching them how to enjoy a job well done.

Each Wednesday night, Charlie had the boys come to the store after hours and stock the shelves with the weekly delivery. After they finished with the chores, Charlie rewarded them by taking them into the basement, where he had set up a makeshift shooting range.

They were carefully instructed on how to care for and shoot a .32-caliber Smith & Wesson revolver. Charlie occasionally took them out to the fields for rabbit hunting with this same pistol. Later, Bob had an old .22 rifle that occasionally jammed. Bob was aware of this and was extremely careful when he used it. One time, Dale borrowed Bob's rifle to target shoot without permission, and Dale ended up carelessly shooting himself in the foot.

Although Charlie was looked upon as a much-needed father figure for the boys, he eventually spent less time with both Bob's mom and her family. The time he spent with them became a lifelong memory to Bob of what a father and son relationship should feel like.

Bob was more inclined to mechanical tasks rather than schoolwork. He was always an outgoing and social individual but was often disciplined at school and became tired of the school's restrictive environment. During once such occurrence, Bob was subject to a corporal punishment session. Bob grabbed the paddle from the school teacher, threw it across the room, and headed out the door.

When Bob mustered the courage to return to school a few days later, the principal and a male teacher tried to corner Bob to once again inflict the prescribed punishment. He pushed his way through the two adults and escaped out a side door.

Upon his return to school a week later near the end of the school year, Bob informed the principal that he would no longer be subject to paddling at school. The principal informed him that he was going to be advanced to the eighth grade but that Bob still needed to adhere by the authority of that school if he chose to return. Bob finished the year without additional incidents but chose to not return the following school year.

The oldest brother, Larry, went off to the service in 1951. He is pictured with his mom and her longtime suitor, Charlie.

Working at Age 13

Since he was no longer attending school, Bob constantly searched for ways to work and raise money. He realized that the common light-metal lattice radio antenna towers were often aged and rusty in appearance. He went around town and offered to paint the towers (the average height was 30 feet) with silver paint for 25 cents per foot. He could make $7.50 in a single day.

It was a lot of work to paint all edges and surfaces of the intricate towers, as they were not designed to support the weight of a full-grown man. Bob fit the bill well with the work ethic of an adult but the size and energy of a young teen. This became a good warm-weather business for Bob—one that he could accomplish between his morning and afternoon paper routes while other kids his age were attending school.

The largest tower he was asked to paint was 96 feet tall. A friend named Kevin offered to pay Bob $30 for this service. At 13 years old, Bob

Bob bought and fixed up cars in his spare time. He purchased cars (such as this near-perfect 1949 Oldsmobile convertible) that had mechanical issues, did the repairs, and enjoyed the car. After some time, he sold the car for a profit and began the process over again.

began painting high on the tower with Kevin working below him. While moving his paint bucket, Bob accidentally tipped it over and spilled most of its contents over Kevin's head and face. Although there were a few choice words, Kevin still paid Bob the agreed-upon compensation at the job's completion.

Virgil Cates was one of Bob's friends, and Virgil's father owned a junkyard in town. Even before Bob had a license, he worked for Virgil Sr. and was paid to pull parts for customers. Virgil Sr. took a liking to Bob, and as Bob approached the age of 16, Virgil purchased a 1940 Chevrolet for the wrecking yard for $25. The owner had complained of a terrible clunk in the drivetrain and suspected that the transmission had failed. Virgil Sr. showed Bob how to change out the driveline and install a new U-joint, and the noise went away. Bob was given this as his first car in place of wages.

Not long after Bob earned his driver's license, he took the car downtown on the way to Isaly's for ice cream. As he was turning into the parking lot, he was hit head-on by a man on a Harley-Davidson, and it totaled the 1940 Chevrolet. Both Bob and the man riding the motorcycle were unhurt. Bob replaced the 1940 Chevy with a 1947 Ford that had a flathead V-8 and 3-speed transmission. Although it was stock, Bob tuned it to perfection, which frustrated one friend in particular. John Morrow just couldn't keep up with his similarly equipped 1946 Ford coupe. Soon, Bob was being paid by his friends to tune their flathead Fords.

Working at a Business

The cost to maintain his car soon required additional income. So, at 17 years old, Bob finally gave up the paper route when he was hired by the company Flxible in Loudonville, Ohio, just 20 miles southeast of Mansfield. Flxible had started to build buses for a new Chicago Transit Authority order.

Bob worked the graveyard shift each night and drove the 20 miles one way from his home in Mansfield. He was hired as a riveter and worked to attach the bus body panels and floors on the assembly line. It was hard work, especially with Bob trying to keep a normal social life during the day when his coworkers had learned to rest.

Returning home to Mansfield late one night, Bob fell asleep at the wheel and woke up to the car plowing into a field, where it finally came to a stop by rolling over. Bob pulled it out of the dirt and was able to repair the fenders and roof of the car so that he could continue to use it. During the year that Bob worked at Flxible, he learned to appreciate working a normal daytime schedule.

Bob returned to a regular daytime work schedule when he joined Brandenburg Chevrolet in Mansfield at 18 years old. He liked the fact that this was a day job, which allowed him time to once again interact with his friends in the evenings and on weekends.

As a line mechanic, Bob was trained extensively in general automotive repair, but it was soon discovered that he excelled with performance tune-ups. In less than a year, the general manager noticed Bob's social nature, observed how well he interacted with the customers, and promoted him to be the dealership's service writer.

With Bob's oldest brother, Larry, off to the service, Dale and Bob remained close. Here, Bob holds Dale while playing baseball at the small field down the street from their home in Mansfield.

Bob has owned numerous cars over the years, but he most fondly remembers his 1949 Oldsmobile convertible, which was purchased for the princely sum of $800 due to a troubling ticking noise coming from the engine. The car was in brand-new condition except for the anticipated extensive repair to bearings or upper valvetrain. After talking with other more experienced mechanics, Bob performed a quick oil change with the addition of a can of Alemite CD-2, and the noisy engine quieted down permanently.

Many of Bob's friends envied him and offered to purchase the luxurious Oldsmobile 88 convertible. Over time, Bob finally succumbed to his brother Dale and allowed him to buy the magnificent drop-top.

During this time, both of Bob's brothers (Dale and Larry) were serving in the US Navy. Larry had entered at age 15 with the help of his mother, and Dale enlisted in 1954 at age 20. While in the service, Larry married and moved to Chicago, never to move back to the Mansfield area. Even with Dale stationed 2,000 miles away on the West Coast, Dale and Bob remained close. This tight brotherly relationship kept them involved in the automotive business together for many years.

Spreading His Wings

By age 20, Bob moved 80 miles away from Mansfield to the big city of Cleveland. His great-aunt May offered to take him in, and he started doing mechanical repairs and tune-ups at an auto repair shop on Rocky River Drive. During this time, Chevrolet introduced the 1955 Bel Air with the 265 V-8 engine that Bob learned to performance tune for the local hot rodders. He remained in Cleveland for a few years and performed other tasks, including body shop work.

In the late 1950s, Bondo was introduced in place of metal and lead for body repairs. Bob felt that the chemicals released by the new body filler were unsafe for the workers and chose to head back to Mansfield and open his own repair shop.

In 1958, Bob started D&B Automotive on Diamond Street in Mansfield with Doug, a local friend. They specialized in performing V-8 engine swaps for older 6-cylinder cars. Later, when Doug chose to work for a different shop, Bob's brother Dale joined in working together at D&B Automotive.

Between engine swaps, Bob helped a friend from Cleveland with his home roofing business. Always the prankster, Bob was on a roof one day and noticed a large pile of loose sand just below where he was working. He pretended to fall off the roof and landed on the soft sand. The roofer ran over concerned for his safety to find Bob laughing hysterically at the joke.

Soon, Bob tried his hand at running his own roofing company. He rented a building in south Mansfield on Diamond Street for $85 a month. He successfully continued the business for a short time until the D&B garage business picked up enough to become his primary income.

Neighborhood Demolition Derby

Old beat-up cars were easy for Bob and his friends to find, and dent and rust repairs were not high on the priority list for their winter cars. Bob and his friends often inflicted damage when they encountered each other at stoplights. They would reach out of their car and hit their friend's winter beater, creating a new dent on the roof with the assistance of a tire iron. These competitive challenges also included the

On Easter Sunday in 1955, 20-year-old Bob and 21-year-old Dale prepare to go to church in Bob's 1950 Ford.

occasional low-speed intentional bumper tapping.

On one rambunctious occasion in 1960, Bob and his friends Dave Billman and "Squeege" Darrel Jerger met on the streets of Ashland, Ohio. Bob asked his two friends to park very close together at the local hamburger joint. Then, Bob attempted to park between his two friends' cars, intentionally damaging both. Broken mirrors and trim littered the parking lot. Onlookers thought this was accidental, but the threesome had planned it from the start.

From the parking lot skirmish, the trio chose to turn the day into an all-out demolition derby in a vacant parcel behind Dave's used car lot next door. Always the competitor, Bob continued to demolish the straight-8 Buick until all body panels were crumpled and most of the glass was broken out. They destroyed both 1957 Fords and the 1948 Buick sedan, but in the end, Bob was declared the winner.

Racing for Others

For a short time, Bob raced a 1940 Willys coupe that had a modern Buick Nailhead 322-ci V-8, Hilborn fuel injection, and a heavy-duty LaSalle 3-speed transmission. During a final run in the A/Gas category, Bob was 500 feet down the track when the hood flew open, which cracked the windshield and dented the roof. Bob stuck his head out the window and continued to shift and drive the remainder of the quarter-mile for the win. Little did he know that this was an omen for his upcoming professional racing career when he would pilot the *Hemi Under Glass*.

Bob soon built a reputation as a good driver and was hired to drive a dirt track car for Mr. Huffman.

Friends Dave, Squeege, and Bob relax after an impromptu demolition derby in a local vacant lot. Both the 1957 Ford hardtop and the 1948 Buick four-door car were heavily damaged during the afternoon event. Even though the cars were totaled, the engines were saved for future hot rod projects.

Bob stands proud and victorious next to his destroyed Buick. The damage to the roof was created in town prior to the afternoon dent fest. The big Buick was still mobile after receiving a multitude of damage.

While racing this dirt track car, Bob ran into and ruptured the other racer's fuel tank. The fuel spewed over Bob and his car. He immediately stopped and stripped off his fire suit. Luckily no fire began and he escaped unharmed.

He drove in local weekend races around Mansfield and Ashland for two seasons. Bob was involved in a race when the steering broke as he went into a corner, sending him straight off the track and into the field below.

As Bob walked back up the hill onto the track, the announcer was surprised to see Bob on foot because no one had noticed that he was no longer racing with the others. During another race, Bob was soaked with gas when another car lost its gas tank in front of him and he couldn't avoid running it over. Bob was able to safely stop and exit the vehicle, but the situation pointed out the lack of safety involved in the dirt track racing environment.

Meeting Nanci

At age 25 in 1960, Bob met his future wife when he delivered a car that he serviced to an employee at a local office building. He saw Nanci walking across the parking lot and thought to himself, "Now, there is a girl that I need to get to know."

Bob was not timid. He acted on the opportunity to ask her out but was promptly turned down. Bob left

The hood flew up and smashed into the roof of this Willys mid-race. Bob never let up on the gas and won his round despite having to look around the obstruction.

feeling rejected, but Nanci's coworkers knew Bob and pointed out to her that he was a hard worker and owned his own repair business. The fact that he was tall and handsome was also seen as a positive characteristic.

Bob made sure to stop by Nanci's work often, and she finally consented to a lunch date. The reluctant lunch date turned into a second date, and soon, most of their free time was being spent together. It didn't take long before they both knew that this relationship was meant to be. After a brief courtship, they were engaged and promptly married at the First Lutheran Church in Mansfield with their friends and family in attendance.

At age 25, Bob was newly married and soon anticipating the birth of his first son. He was the owner of D&B Automotive and busy doing engine swaps for local young men who wanted more performance in their hot rods. Bob was involved in transplanting modern large-displacement motors out of wrecked cars into Tri-Five Chevys. His transplant engine of choice was either the very common small-block Chevrolet or the more elusive and powerful 389 Pontiac motors.

Bob owned a 1955 Chevrolet that he had re-powered with an early 1960s Pontiac 389 Tri-Power with a Corvette 4-speed transmission. Although the car was quick and helped create a strong reputation for Bob on the street, he chose to increase its horsepower by combining two separate Tri-Power setups into a custom-built six-carb manifold system. All of this power was hidden under a plain-Jane 1955 Chevrolet two-door post. Complete with hubcaps and whitewall tires, Bob drove this sleeper around town to troll for unsuspecting street racers.

One of the hot rods that Bob built at D&B was a green '55 Chevy 210 two-door post sedan with a transplanted 389 Pontiac Tri-Power V-8. Bob was racing against a friend's '57 Chevy with a hopped-up 283 V-8 that Bob had constructed for him. Bob had his friends Cliff Cross and Willie Altaffer as passengers in the '55 Chevy. The '57 Chevy lost traction and veered into the quarter panel of the '55, which caused the car to turn sideways and go into the ditch, where it rolled over multiple times.

This was long before seat belts were standard equipment on cars, and all three were hurt and required a trip to the hospital. Cliff's injuries were the most severe with a broken neck and skull fracture. Bob recalled that Cliff's head was shaved, he received over 200 stitches, and he had to wear a neck brace. The young men had so many visitors in the hospital that the older roommate complained. Bob snuck in a pint of whiskey for the hospital roommate to make up for all the noise created by the youth.

Westward Ho

Dale remained in California until 1969, when he left the navy. In 1962, after spending Christmas with Dale in San Jose, Bob and friend Angelo Mariatti were driving home in Angelo's new 1962 Corvair Monza.

As they headed east outside of Albuquerque, New Mexico, Bob and Angelo had to dodge a rolling object on the highway. Upon closer

Bob's wife, Nanci, (left) and his mother and younger sister, Beverly, celebrate Easter Sunday at their mom's home in Mansfield.

Bob poses with a friend at the Shell station where he worked. Bob later purchased the local Pure Oil station in Mansfield.

The rear fender of the 1955 Chevrolet was hit by the other car while the two were racing, which pushed the car sideways and off the road.

The 1955 Chevrolet landed on the passenger's door during one of the barrel rolls, which caused injuries to all three occupants.

Every panel of the Chevrolet was damaged. Even the sturdy frame was twisted, which rendered the car unsalvageable. Bob removed the Pontiac 389 Tri-Power motor and transmission and installed it in another 1955 Chevrolet.

The Pontiac 389 Tri-Power motor was salvaged from the damaged Green 1955 Chevy. Bob is preparing it for the next transplant procedure.

Bob and his friends placed the Pontiac motor into another 1955 Chevrolet two-door sedan. One friend is jokingly using a pitchfork to assist in the installation.

inspection, they discovered it was a frozen holiday turkey. They stopped and put it in the trunk (front) of the little Corvair. After a few more miles, they stopped and retrieved another. A short distance later, they discovered a frozen ham. Within a few miles, they gathered three turkeys and two hams that they shared

If three carburetors are good, then six must be better. Bob had two Tri-Power setups combined into a six carburetor, which resulted in 12 barrels of fuel delivery for the 389-ci engine. With a little special tuning and dual exhausts, the car was hard to beat during street races.

Bob poses with his Chevrolet and a friend's Studebaker Hawk. The Chevrolet kept its sleeper status with wide whitewall tires and full hubcaps. Only the custom grille ornament gave notice that the car was a wolf in sheep's clothing.

Bob's friends sit on a typical Model A hot rod with a transplanted modern V-8 engine at the Shell station in Mansfield.

with family once they returned home. The additional weight over the front tires assisted the Corvair's steering on the snow-covered Ohio highways.

Bob was active in all forms of racing and purchased a Norsecraft boat and a brand-new 100-hp Mercury outboard motor. Over the years he owned this boat, he accumulated a group of trophies from races around the Central Ohio region.

Bob enjoyed his visit to California with the mountain ranges and varying terrain. A short time after getting married, Bob was offered a job to work as a maintenance mechanic at a gold mining camp out in Quincy, California. Bob and Nanci were enticed by the adventure, and they chose to accept the job offer and move. Located in the mountains of northern California, Bob and Nanci drove their 1957 Chrysler with its 396 Hemi out West with the race boat in tow.

On Bucks Lake in Quincy, California, Nanci wanted to drive the boat. With Bob in the passenger's seat instructing her, she hit the throttle a little too quickly and almost put the boat on its tail. With a little more practice, Nanci was clocked at 63 mph that day. For the year that Nanci and Bob lived in Quincy, Nanci worked with the county attorney and was responsible for the law library at the courthouse.

Also while in Quincy, Bob successfully prepared the powerplant to perform multiple tasks at one time. This allowed the plant to be more productive and use the same power unit as before but in a more efficient way.

Bob purchased a Norsecraft boat and a brand-new 100-hp Mercury outboard motor to try his hand at boat racing.

Bob poses with the road trophies that he and friend Angelo Mariatti found along the road in New Mexico. They fell out of a moving truck that drove in front of them along the backroad highway.

By the time that they had retrieved the frozen turkeys and a few hams, the front trunk of the little Corvair was overloaded by the weight.

Bob's short career in boat racing proved to be a successful endeavor. Here, he sits in the boat with a bevy of trophies that he acquired during the summer racing season.

Newlyweds Bob and Nanci stand in front of their 1957 Chrysler that had a 392 Hemi. Little did Bob know how important the Hemi engine would become later in his career.

Nanci was a bit of a speed demon in her own right. While in northern California, she enjoyed driving the Norsecraft boat with the Mercury outboard motor to a new record of 63 mph.

While Bob was away from the camp one day, two coworkers failed to clean the crushed ore off of the floor as required. This allowed the hot stone to catch the facility on fire. The forest service responded to the fire but was only able to keep the fire from spreading into the surrounding forest. Without a plant to run, Bob and Nanci returned home to Ohio.

This was the little mining camp in northern California where Bob and Nanci lived during their first year of marriage. Bob was the lead mechanic and kept all of the required machinery operational for the gold mining operation.

Chapter 2

Hurst Creates a Racer

George Hurst was a celebrity in his own right at the racetrack. Here, he clowns around with well-known comedian Ernest Borgnine. (Photo Courtesy Mark Fletcher Collection)

The brand we know as Hurst began in 1958 as Hurst/Campbell at George Hurst's kitchen table with engineer Bill Campbell. The initial business was centered around putting high-performance V-8 motors in older vehicles. George created a rough design of motor-mount plates that allowed hot rodders to safely install Chevrolet V-8s in a variety of cars with a minimum of welding.

Young Bill Campbell answered an advertisement placed by George Hurst in the local Pennsylvania newspaper that asked for an engineer and draftsman. Soon, Bill documented and continued to improve George's original designs. The engineering drawings were utilized to create a system for consistent production, which enabled more sales of the motor-mount conversion kits.

The business soon included a precision floor-mounted, 3-speed shifter that was favored by both the racing professional and hobbyist. George's ideas and marketing finesse coupled with Bill's obsession with engineering detail allowed the burgeoning company to create the benchmark in performance shifters.

By 1964, Hurst was a household name to young gearheads who looked for ways to make their cars faster. George Hurst was constantly marketing the Hurst/Campbell

Hurst-Campbell Inc. was formed in 1958 between George Hurst and Bill Campbell. The business consisted of making and selling engineered motor conversion kits with a shop that did the conversion for wealthy clients. (Photo Courtesy Mark Fletcher Collection)

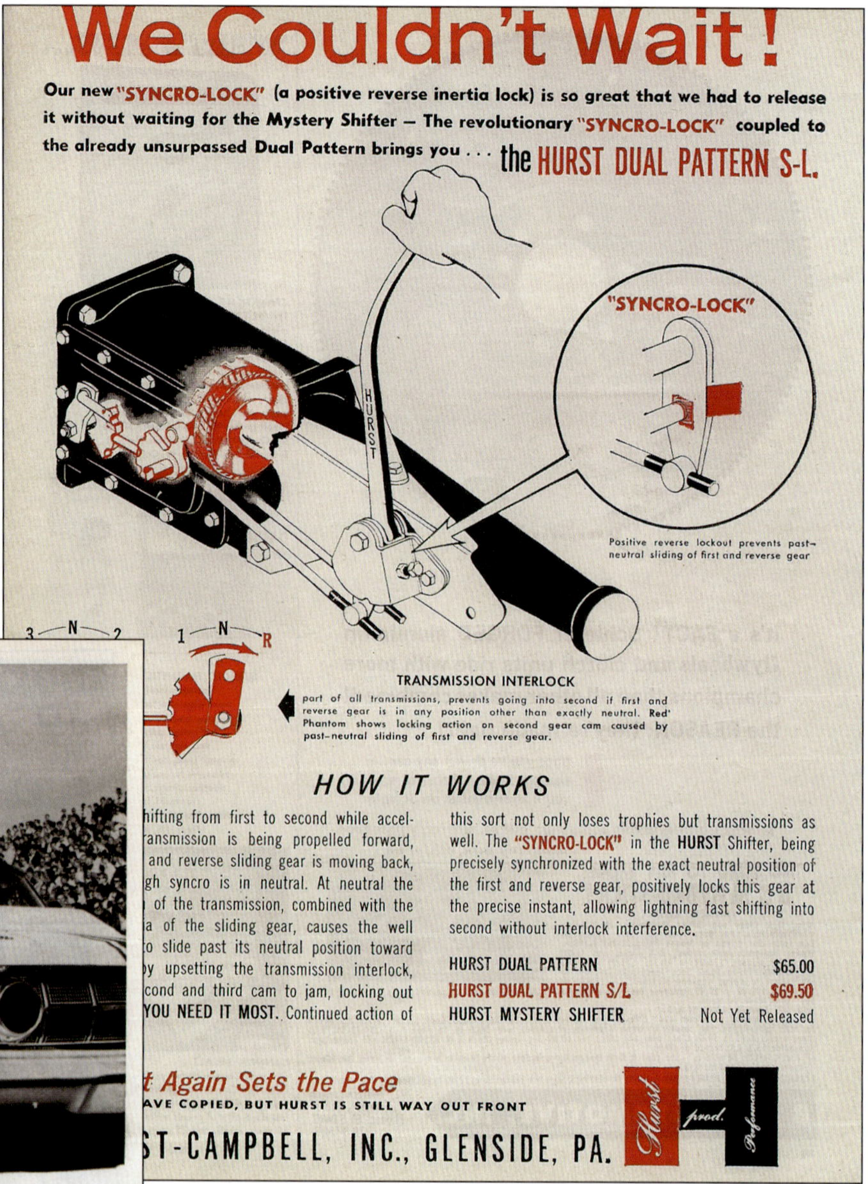

In 1963, Hurst introduced the Synchro-Lock Hurst dual-pattern shifter that virtually eliminated the accidental shifting into reverse while performance driving. The heavy spring design kept the driver from unintentionally moving the shifter into reverse without applying a specific movement into the gate. (Photo Courtesy Mark Fletcher Collection)

Hurst sponsorship was promoted in full-page ads in Hot Rod *and other performance magazines.*

brand by sponsoring races and providing lavish awards. These sponsorships not only awarded prize money for each winner but also included a new car and other valuable prizes for the top contenders at the season's finale event.

Hurst also supported the racers by having employees present at each major race event with a service truck equipped with all the necessary tools. The Hurst team helped repair any racers' cars that broke during the elimination races. This assistance was provided at no charge, but the racers paid Hurst back with a fierce loyalty for Hurst company products.

With the introduction of the Hurst floor shifters, Hurst became a major sponsor to most automotive racing venues. In 1964, Hurst sponsored the Indianapolis NHRA National drag racing event with cash awards and a set of four crew uniforms for the top team. (Photo Courtesy Mark Fletcher Collection)

Hurst created a small fleet of repair trucks that attended major races around the country. This early 1-ton Dodge truck was equipped to sell and install shifters for competitors attending the race. On-the-spot repairs of all kinds were performed to keep the drag racers in the competition. Hurst performed these repairs at no cost to those entered in the race. (Photo Courtesy Mark Fletcher Collection)

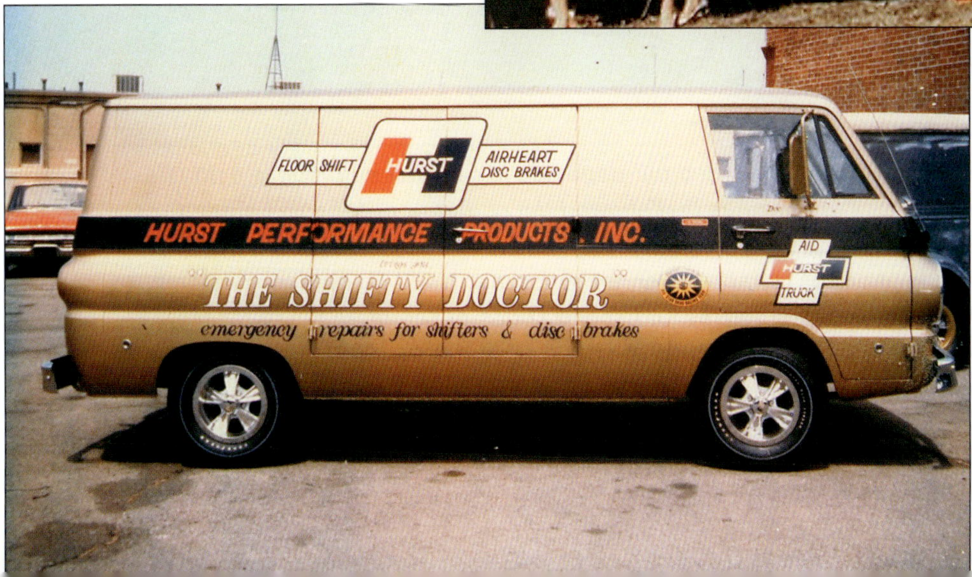

Hurst created a multitude of smaller Hurst Aid vans over the years. The gold and black 1968 Dodge panel van was a common sight in the race pits. (Photo Courtesy Mark Fletcher Collection)

Mystery Shifter

Racers soon understood that the Hurst components were solidly engineered and the best-built performance accessories they could buy, which further solidified the marriage between racing and the Hurst brand.

With Hurst's phenomenal success came a series of challenges. Multiple lower-cost competitors entered into the floor shifter market

Bill Campbell (seated) and George Hurst discuss a Hurst Competition Plus shifter with car models on the desk. The largest is the ill-fated 1964 Hurst Shifter Special Indy car. The Hemi Under Glass *is posed doing a wheel-stand. The third is a model of George Hurst's personal car, a front-wheel-drive 1966 Oldsmobile Toronado customized with a factory Tri-Power carburetion system and see-through plexiglass hood scoop. (Photo Courtesy Mark Fletcher Collection)*

Hurst created full-page ads in national automotive enthusiast magazines that showed the shifter applications it made for specific cars. The earliest ads included prices and mail-order information. As the Hurst reseller network grew, Hurst pointed the customer to local parts houses and speed shops to complete the purchase. (Photo Courtesy Mark Fletcher Collection)

Hurst offered multiple versions of floor shifter models designed to convert steering-column-mounted shifters to the floor. Others converted a sloppy factory OEM shifter to precise performance shifter hardware. (Photo Courtesy Mark Fletcher Collection)

Hurst was not satisfied with only selling performance shifters over the speed shop counter to the performance-minded owners. In 1965, Hurst 4-speed shifters were factory installed in the new Plymouth Barracuda. In 1966, the Oldsmobile 4-4-2 equipped with a manual transmission also came from the manufacturer with a Hurst shifter that had "442" emblazoned vertically on the sides. (Photo Courtesy Mark Fletcher Collection)

and created some erosion to sales. To keep customers from defecting to these competitors, George announced a lower-cost shifter with most of the features of Hurst's current offerings. The new product was quickly labeled the "Mystery Shifter" because George began to promote and take orders for it before it was fully engineered. The recipe was simply to remove manufacturing costs so that it could retail for half of Hurst's existing product line.

Bill Campbell identified that the heavy, flat handles that were designed specifically for each vehicle were the most expensive individual component after the complicated shifter mechanism. By using an adjustable-height, round handle with simple bends in combination with adjustable-length shifting rods, engineering met the cost-reduction goals with a minimum of different part numbers.

This product was extremely successful as an entry-level shifter for aspiring racers whose limited income dictated the choice. The Mystery Shifter quickly filled the void between the standard car manufacturer's offerings and Hurst's top-of-the-line product.

In the spring of 1963, discussions ensued that culminated in the Hurst shifter becoming standard on 4-speed-equipped models of Pontiac's GTO for 1964. For the first year of the new GTO, the shifter was

By the mid-1960s, Hurst's shifter production line produced 95 percent of the company's sales. Hurst-Campbell was a well-known product name in the automotive aftermarket business. (Photo Courtesy Mark Fletcher Collection)

Linda Vaughn joined Hurst as the Miss Hurst Shifter in 1965. She quickly became an ambassador for the company and attended most major racing events to represent Hurst. Linda remembers people and their names, which makes everyone whom she meets feel important. (Photo Courtesy Mark Fletcher Collection)

built and supplied by Hurst but not labeled as being Hurst. In comparison, during the same model year, the sporty new 1964 Barracuda came with a Hurst-labeled 4-speed shifter.

George Hurst's longtime friend Jim Wangers felt that Pontiac was missing the marketing advantage related to the strength of the Hurst name. Through subsequent meetings with GM executives Pete Estes, Bunkie Knudsen, and John DeLorean, for the 1965 Pontiac GTO production, the Hurst name was prominently cast into the side of the shifter for all to see. Wangers made sure that the Hurst name remained on every Pontiac manufactured with a Hurst shifter since that first year.

Hurst production was in full swing, and by this time George and partner Bill worked out of three separate buildings in the Glenside, Pennsylvania, area. They developed a plan to reduce costs and create a more efficient manufacturing process by bringing all operations into a single location. A new 100,000-square-foot facility was built in nearby Warminster, Pennsylvania, on a 20-acre site directly across from the Johnsville Naval Base where George was last stationed during his service career.

The facility opened among much fanfare generated by the flamboyant George Hurst and a growing company marketing team. It was dedicated on January 7, 1965, to the late John Bonner, a longtime friend and insurance salesman who assisted George and Bill to make their partnership official at George's kitchen table back in 1958.

The Hurst team had become actively involved with OEM projects for both Pontiac and Chrysler and needed a Detroit-area facility where Hurst could directly interface with engineers from each company. Because they were often working on cars before public release, there was a required measure of security. For its Pontiac-related projects, Hurst had used the service facility at Ace

Wilson's Royal Pontiac in Royal Oak, but the automotive press was on to Royal Pontiac's strategic position within Pontiac and information was often leaked.

To solve this problem and facilitate additional OEM projects, Hurst opened the Hurst Performance Research Center in Madison Heights, Michigan. It served as a skunkworks of sorts with a portion of the shop segregated to maintaining security among the different manufacturers' projects. There were times when competing car manufacturers had prototype vehicles in the same building within 30 feet of each other without ever being the wiser.

When not being used for official business, these shop areas were commonly used by OEM engineers for customizing their personal or company-provided cars. These cars were often involved in head-to-head brand match races on nearby Woodward Avenue.

George Hurst enjoyed his role as a dignitary and sponsor for many racing venues. In late 1965, he looked for a new Miss Hurst Golden Shifter to replace Janene Walsh and Pat Flannery. In normal flamboyant George fashion, he placed an ad in *Hot Rod* magazine and held auditions at three separate racing events.

One of the contestants, Linda Vaughn, was a vivacious young lady who had been both Miss Atlanta International Raceway and Miss Firebird Fuel. She wowed the crowd with her charming personality and a curvaceous figure that seemed to never hold still. George was easily enthralled by this young and talented lady. She not only won the contest but she also soon became one of the first female ambassadors to the historically male-dominated sport of auto racing.

There Is No Need for a Rearview Mirror on a Race Car

Drag racing and Hurst-Campbell both came of age during the early 1960s, first in connection to car owners putting modern V-8 engines in prewar bodies and frames when creating their hot rods. As drag racing continued to grow, the sanctioning bodies added more classes, and match racing gained a following by equalizing the exhibitions with dial-in times.

The local tracks discovered that drivers would pay to participate, and their friends would pay to watch. As the sport grew, the local tracks began to attract participants from an ever-expanding regional area. By introducing more professional racers from out of the area, the crowds grew to support their favorite local competitors over the big guns from out of town. The private track owners knew this and were inclusive of multiple categorized classes to attract the biggest crowds. For the price of a movie, spectators could enjoy an evening of racing that incorporated all of the five senses with wild fluctuations of one's pulse.

Most tracks were family owned and only operated seasonally.

Linda Vaughn's contributions to the Hurst brand can't be understated. For more than a decade, she had nearly 300 appearances annually. She promoted Hurst Shifters at trade shows, dealership appearances, and nearly every form of automobile racing imaginable. (Photo Courtesy Linda Vaughn Collection)

The Hurst team motored around the events on mini bikes or golf carts. Here, Linda laughs while being escorted around.

The Hurst Aid vehicles carried fuel and parts in support of the* Hairy Olds *and* Hemi Under Glass *exhibition vehicles. (Photo Courtesy Marty Danko Collection)

Given the possibility of inclement weather, the season would start around Memorial Day and typically continue through Labor Day weekend. If the tracks were located in the Southwest, they continued to run into the late fall and drew sufficient crowds to fill the grandstands. Because of its location in Southern California and its proximity to the huge Los Angeles market, the Pomona, California, track was established as the venue for the annual Winternationals starting in 1961.

Soon, the track owners learned to promote special events to attract both racers and spectators with a winner's purse that ranged from $20 for a class win to $1,000 for an event win. Companies such as Hurst-Campbell and other suppliers sponsored many of the purses as a form of advertising. They often included additional cash bonuses for anyone who won their class with a car equipped with their respective companies' products.

At these events, Hurst promoted its products and its brand through the Hurst Doctor at the major events. Hurst had a fleet of trucks, trailers, tools, and employees who would set up in the pits and help the participating racers fix their cars when something broke. It was a brilliant strategy. Hurst also assisted participants by selling and installing its products right at the track.

As the 1960s progressed and the popularity of drag racing grew, each of the tracks competed for spectators within each region and looked for unique ways to stand out among competing tracks.

Hurst used the events to display its growing number of products as it brought in companies like Schiefer clutches and Airheart brake components.

Hurst Sponsorships

Larger purses and more amenities helped draw larger fields, which in turn drew more spectators. Soon, the track owners offered to pay Hurst and other sponsors to attend their events. Although these payments or concessions did not fully offset Hurst's costs to participate, the symbiotic relationship helped grow Hurst's sales by the middle of the decade.

Jack Duffy worked for Hurst as its public relations manager. He and his team scheduled the Hurst Shifty Doctor's attendance at the requested events. Although Jack Duffy was popular among the racers, he was not well-known to the public. His most public appearances were at the wheel of the Hurst convertibles that were utilized to drive Miss Hurst Golden Shifter, Linda Vaughn, around the track as she stood on a large platform and clung to an oversized Hurst shifter.

Hurst Floor Shift Special

Hurst looked for more high-profile ways to promote the growing company and create automotive history in the process. In 1964, he partnered with the legendary Smokey Yunick who had developed an unusual chassis for the

PROMOTIONAL ITEMS

JACKET PATCHES — Thousands already wear these handsomely styled colored Hurst patches . . . identifying themselves with Hurst Performance Products . . .

(1) BIG 8-INCH DIAMETER EMBLEM DESIGNED TO FIT ON THE BACK OF ANY JACKET, SWEAT SHIRT, REGULAR SHIRT. (2) 5 INCH DIAMETER EMBLEM FITS ON FRONT OR JACKET SLEEVE, SWEAT SHIRT OR REGULAR SHIRT.

(3) HURST PERFORMANCE DECAL featuring the famous Hurst trademark in black and bright red. (4) A Hurst shifter is featured on this big 6 inch diameter pressure-sensitive decal.

(5) CRAZY DECAL is what we tag this cartoon-style "Stick Decal." It's a real screamer — 4 inches high.

(6) MOTOR MOUNT DECAL — also cartoon style.

(7) T-SHIRTS SUIT THE RACE FRATERNITY TO A T! . . . Available in small, medium, large and extra large. Finest quality cotton, with striking non-fade Hurst emblem in front.

(8) BEWARE DECAL . . . warns all comers that you are equipped with the world's finest floor shift. Here's a 4-inch high "status symbol," for any and all cars.

(9) HURST ON YOUR HEAD . . . with this bright yellow, red and black bordered cap sporting a fine cloth "H" up front. Sizes: Small, medium, large and extra large.

(10) DASH WARNING STICKER. it's 3¼ x 1¾ inches pressure sensitive label for your dash. Metallic gold background with red and black lettering. Three and/or four speed shift patterns available.

(11) SWIFTER SHIFTER GLOVE what the well dressed performance man wears with pride. Palm has special gripping material; back is perforated, breathable. Right hand and left hand glove $3.50 each or $5.95 a pair. Sizes: Regular, large and extra large.

(12) TIE TACKS with a ¾ inch reproduction of the Hurst "H" and a Hurst dual pattern makes an attractive tie tack. Individually packed in handsome black box. Lapel Pin also available.

(13) LINE/LOC Decal — also cartoon style. Showing how effective our Line/Loc kit is in preventing car movement.

(14) FIRE BALL Decal (4 speed) shows that you have picked the "Choice of Champions" shifter for your car.

(15) DUAL GATE Decal . . . featuring the famous Hurst "Key" to real driving pleasure. Large and small decal at one low price.

(16) HURST CHOICE OF CHAMPIONS — The HURST A-Go-Go Gal is a real attention getter. (3½" x 4¼").

(17) HYDRO-GATE DECAL — New — our latest and wildest Cartoon Style Decal showing our latest product. (3½" x 6½").

PRICES AND SPECIFICATIONS SUBJECT TO CHANGE WITHOUT NOTICE

HURST PERFORMANCE PRODUCTS, INC.

50 WEST STREET ROAD • WARMINSTER, PENNSYLVANIA 18974

(1) $3.50 LIST PRICE; (2) $2.00 LIST PRICE; (3) .10 LIST PRICE; (4) .25 LIST PRICE; (5) .15 LIST PRICE; (7) $1.95 LIST PRICE; (9) $1.95 LIST PRICE; (11) $3.50 LIST PRICE, SPECIAL PRICE PER PAIR $5.95, RIGHT & LEFT HAND; (12) $3.50 LIST PRICE; (13) .25 LIST PRICE; (14) .20 LIST PRICE; (15) .15 LIST PRICE; (16) .35 LIST PRICE; (17) .25 LIST PRICE

HPP-A-1060-2

Hurst sold race clothing and related items to the spectators at the events attended by the exhibition cars. It was common to see Hurst hats and jackets in the stands during many events.

1964 Indianapolis 500, the *Hurst Floor Shift Special*. This space-age configuration held the driver in a pod similar to a motorcycle sidecar suspended between the left-side tires.

The concept was driven by a 252-ci, naturally aspirated dual overhead cam (DOHC) 4-cylinder Offenhauser engine. It is unclear if Hurst had any input into the unusual design, but both Yunick and Hurst were convinced that an asymmetrical design, enhanced by the driver's weight bias, would revolutionize the sport. The car was painted in black and gold, which were Yunick's standard colors and what became the signature color combination for Hurst.

The car was piloted by Duane Carter Sr. and rookie Bobby Johns, who both tested the car extensively throughout May 1964 in preparation for the Memorial Day race. The concept received extensive media attention during the testing with wild speculation as to whether the design had any scientific or engineering merit. During an attempt to qualify the car, Johns lost control and slid the car backward into the outside wall of Turn 1 and severely damaged it, removing it from further contention. No subsequent attempt was made to race the car again.

The car was repaired and kept as part of the Indianapolis Motor Speedway Hall of Fame Museum. It was also loaned out to the Honda Museum in Motegi, Japan, and has been shown at the 2010 Amelia Island Concourse de Elegance event.

George, undaunted by the failure of this experiment, was encouraged by the overwhelming publicity for the failed Indy effort. He immediately jumped into another oddity that made a lasting impression on the US racing world.

Hemi Under Glass

The idea was to increase the visibility of the Hurst name at the races. Instead of each car displaying a small sponsor decal mixed in with many others on the side of the car, Hurst wanted the company name emblazoned in 3-foot letters on the side of an exhibition car at each race. It had to be something spectacular that would get the crowds to stop and stare. The new A/FX classification was designed for manufacturer experimental cars, which was the category that had the public and the car magazines talking.

While traveling with Ray Brock just before Christmas, George sketched an idea that combined two new Plymouth product offerings for 1964. He used a bowling alley lounge napkin to show the concept of combining the new Barracuda with the 426 supercharged race Hemi. The engine bay was too small to host the massive elephant motor, so George suggested moving the motor to the back of the car where there was plenty of room under the huge back window that was used to add fastback styling to Plymouth's compact Valiant.

Hurst told Brock that he wanted to create an FX car for the following season, similar to the Mercury Comets and Pontiac LeMans that ran in 1964. George Hurst drew a Plymouth Barracuda on a napkin with the Hemi in the rear of the car, where the back seat was usually located. To show how intent Hurst was to be competitive with the car, they hired Bill Shrewsberry who had

Hurst's first race car entry was the* Hurst Floor Shift Special*, which was designed with Smokey Yunick to race at Indianapolis in 1964. Driven by Duane Carter Sr., the car had a separate pod for the driver in an attempt to keep a balanced and low center of gravity. The unique car was damaged during pre-race testing and was unable to participate in the Indianapolis 500. (Photo Courtesy Steve Weiner Collection)

Paul Hatton

Paul Hatton was a Detroit-based car painter who specialized in lettering race cars and promotional car signs. Hurst used him to paint the bold red and black *H* on the side of the Hurst Pontiac convertibles that George Hurst used at the racing events. Normally, these vehicles included a platform and oversized shifter that the Hurst girl held onto as the car lapped the track before the races started.

Paul was brought into the Madison Heights Hurst facility at the end of the *Hemi Under Glass* build to letter the black and gold car.

Paul was a talented source that Hurst also used during the build process of the 1968 Hurst Olds, 1969 Hurst Olds, and the 1969 AMC SC/Rambler. For each of these production runs, Paul traveled to Lansing, Michigan, or Kenosha, Wisconsin, to pinstripe the graphics and put the finishing touch on each of the Hurst special cars.

Paul Hatton painted the Hurst lettering on the **Hemi Under Glass**. *Paul was hired by Hurst to pinstripe each of the 1968 and 1969 Hurst Oldsmobiles as well as the 1969 AMC Hurst SC/Ramblers.*

The idea of moving the engine to the rear of the car for added traction was shared by Ray Brock and George Hurst over cocktails and written on a napkin. Hurst created this image for an advertisement to explain the concept for the **Hemi Under Glass**. *For the advertisement, the cocktails were replaced by a cup of coffee. (Photo Courtesy Mark Fletcher Collection)*

been the driver of Jack Chrisman's 1964 Sachs & Sons Mercury Comet Cyclone A/FX.

In the spring of 1965, Hurst approached Chrysler with his idea and soon procured a factory-fresh black 1965 Barracuda. The car was delivered directly from Chrysler to the new Hurst Performance Research Center in Madison Heights, Michigan. A new car-building team was assembled to create

Hurst started the* Hemi Under Glass *project with a standard-production 1965 Plymouth Barracuda provided to Hurst by Chrysler. This photo was staged to represent the massive Hemi motor entering the passenger compartment during the build. (Photo Courtesy Mark Fletcher Collection)

and consisted of Dave Landrith, Jack Watson, Paul Phelps, Dick Chrysler, and others.

While in Hawaii during the fall of 1964, George relentlessly pursued Bill Shrewsberry of Pontiac A/FX fame to get him to drive the new Hemi-powered Barracuda. Bill had been successful with driving the special 1963 Pontiac LeMans 421 drag car for Mickey Thompson and then the 1964 A/FX Comet of Jack Chrisman. They spent a day together at sea, and George outlined the value of relocating the motor into the backseat area and how it would resolve the traction issues plaguing many of the higher-powered drag cars.

The Hurst team was already busy at work re-engineering the little Barracuda. The horsepower and torque of a mighty Hemi V-8 would cause the car's unibody construction to twist and crumble without additional strengthening. The interior flooring was removed, and a new frame was constructed and welded in. This rear frame assembly supported the increased weight of the Elephant Hemi motor, V-Drive assembly, and the rear-end assembly all in a very compact space where the backseat and trunk area were normally be found.

Moving Parts

The construction process was a team effort to insert a huge motor into a tight space. With most of the rear seat and trunk area flooring removed, a square-tube subframe was created to hold the engine and manual transmission through a custom-built V-drive to redirect the torque back to a Corvette independent rear suspension with a transverse leaf spring assembly.

The build was documented as the team made progress. Most of the components required custom fabrication, and the few "off the shelf" parts they used required major modifications to adapt to this creative endeavor.

The completed motor sits directly behind the driver. A steel bulkhead was added to protect the driver should something come apart on the Hemi motor during a high-RPM run. (Photo Courtesy Brian Hatton Collection)

Bostrom seats were used in the A-100 Dodge van and the Ramcharger cars. In an unusual move for a race car, a passenger's seat was added. (Photo Courtesy Brian Hatton Collection)

The engine was initially installed with restrictive dry-element air cleaners that were later switched to velocity stacks. Note that the car retained the rear interior side panels and courtesy lights on the C-pillar. (Photo Courtesy Brian Hatton Collection)

The first independent rear end out of a Corvette design was ill-fated as it proved to be too weak for the monstrous Hemi powerplant. It was soon replaced with a straight-axle design that was better at surviving the tremendous forces of the car. (Photo Courtesy Brian Hatton Collection)

Driver-side rear suspension with double U-joint axles and crossways rear leaf springs were selected to keep the rear wheels in contact with the ground to improve traction and reduce elapsed times. When the car launched, it often lifted all four wheels off the pavement. The rear wheels would still be spinning when they came back down, which grenaded the rear end on the first test day at the track. (Photo Courtesy Brian Hatton Collection)

Hurst employee Dick Chrysler fits the custom-built V-drive housing to the back of the transmission. Fifteen years later, Dick Chrysler purchased the Hurst Corporation. (Photo Courtesy Brian Hatton Collection)

A small fuel tank was fitted to the front of the car for easy access. The Barracuda was equipped with manual steering and a single-chamber brake master cylinder. (Photo Courtesy Brian Hatton Collection)

Looking back through the rear window cavity, the radiator was mounted below the rear trunk lid with no trunk floor below it. (Photo Courtesy Brian Hatton Collection)

Shrewsberry Accepts the Ride

Bill accepted the job, half-thinking that the car would never be built. However, George invited him to Detroit six weeks later for the unveiling of the car. Upon arriving, Shrewsberry immediately identified the

The first **Hemi Under Glass** *performed in Pomona, California, in the spring of 1965. The independent rear suspension quickly failed under the torque of the 425-ci Hemi engine. (Photo Courtesy Steve Weiner Collection)*

Corvette independent rear suspension as the weak link. His intuition was proved to be accurate when it scattered into pieces during his first serious attempt to launch the car.

Not a Race Car

The car was envisioned to be a successful competition racer, but on the first race attempt with a replaced conventional rear axle, Bill stood the car on its rear bumper, and it didn't want to come back down.

With a little practice, Shrewsberry was able to intentionally traverse most of the quarter-mile on the two rear wheels. Bill found that once the car was up, the aerodynamics caused it to stay there until the brakes were applied and the front returned level to the track.

The crowd went wild when the nose of the car stayed in the air. Hurst made lemonade from lemons and started to promote the fact that the car performed unimaginable feats. People often thought there must be some type of trick and wanted to see if the car could do a wheelie for the length of the track. The track promoters realized that the public wanted to be able to get close to touch and inspect the race cars and wheel-standers and allowed for a VIP pass at an additional cost for spectators to view the car in the pits, where they could closely analyze how each car was assembled.

Soon, the public realized the *Hemi Under Glass* did not encompass any mechanical trickery but that it was a result of basic physics and extreme driver skill. During these events that were open to the fans, Bob eagerly interacted with the public, shook hands, and took photos with race fans. He occasionally even allowed fans to sit in the car. His ability to connect with the public

The new Hemi Barracuda is inspected by Hurst employees during its unveiling at the factory facility. Bob Riggle was assigned as lead mechanic for the first year the car was campaigned. (Photo Courtesy Bob Riggle Collection)

Although the* Hemi Under Glass *was anticipated to be a competitor for the new AF/X class, its inability to keep the nose down during hard acceleration made it difficult to steer at speed. (Photo Courtesy Bob Riggle Collection)

The* Hemi Under Glass *was towed to the first year of events behind the company Pontiac. All wheels are Hurst Dazzler wheels designed and sold by Hurst in the 1960s. (Photo Courtesy Bob Riggle Collection)

allowed him to be viewed as a celebrity to the multitude of people who attended.

The Hurst marketing department duties were expanded to include scheduling the *Hurst Hemi Under Glass* to perform exhibition runs at the same major events that Hurst had participated at in the past.

First-Year Improvements

The refined mechanical configuration of the car consisted of a supercharged and injected race-prepped 426 Hemi mated to a Chrysler 4-speed transmission, as it was soon discovered that the dual carbs on the Hemi would run out of fuel before it covered half of the track. A midyear switch to a Hilborn fuel injection system solved the fuel starvation problem.

The power was delivered to the rear wheels through the transmission output directly connected to a V-drive that redirected the force into the rear axle. Originally, the car had no way to be steered once the front wheels were off the ground, so the driver utilized the torque of the motor by feathering the throttle to make minor directional adjustments once in the air. The design of this monster and the experience of driving it soon changed the face of racing and the lives of both its future pilots.

George immediately capitalized on the entertainment value associated with the car and made sure to schedule appearances throughout the race circuit as a paid crowd pleaser. Bill, as the first driver, was compensated with a portion of the proceeds. Out of this, he paid for the travel expenses and overhead for a traveling mechanic. Jack Duffy, the marketing manager at Hurst Corporation, booked the car, which was transported on an open car hauler with Shrewsberry and his mechanic at the wheel. As the car was a rolling advertisement for the new Plymouth Barracuda, the parts required to keep the car running were provided through Chrysler at no cost to Hurst.

Images of the car with its grille pointed toward the sky were used by the tracks in event promotional advertisements. Most events rewarded the team with between $500 and $1,000 per race weekend. At first, the car was christened *A Bear of a Cuda* (Barracuda), but soon it was simply identified as the *Hemi Under Glass*.

Chapter 3

Bob Riggle Joins Hurst

The **Hurst Hairy Hauler** *team is shown at Bakersfield in 1966. George Hurst, June Cochran, Linda Vaughn, Dick Chrysler, and "Doc" Jack Watson were all present. (Photo Courtesy Joe Schubeck Collection)*

When Bob and Nanci returned from the California gold mine back to Mansfield, Ohio, Bob renewed his involvement in his D&B shop to support his young family. During the next four years, the Riggle family grew to four with a fifth on the way. The garage supplied a living for Bob at this time, with some months being good and others being tight for a growing family. In 1965, they had one young son (Jim, age 2) with their second child (Lisa) on the way. A few years down the road, they added another child (Jeff).

Bob was back at D&B auto tuning cars and doing heavy engine replacements for performance-minded drivers. He also continued to race when possible, and he traded his boat for a 1952 Sunbeam Alpine that had been converted to a drag car with a small-block Chevy engine. Bob and his friends traveled to the major races in the Midwest, successfully campaigning the unusual Alpine.

While at the Indianapolis raceway in 1965, Bob and friend Bill Jackson raced an A/Altered car owned by John Hergatt. Bob was wrenching, and Bill was driving well until he was eliminated when he redlighted a race.

That evening, they went to a lounge/restaurant where a band

Young Bob poses like a bodybuilder in this photo taken in his mid-20s. (Photo Courtesy Bob Riggle Collection)

Bob poses with his oldest son, Jim, at their home in Mansfield, Ohio. With one child and another on the way, Bob was happy to be working for Hurst with a regular paycheck to support the growing family.

Young Nanci poses with a painting of her in the early 1960s. Both Bob and Nanci have always remained active and tried to stay healthy over the years.

was playing. Bob asked the waitress to request the band to play the song "Summertime." The waitress returned and stated the band would only play the song if Bob would sing. Bob not only sang "Summertime" but also sang "Red Roses for a Blue Lady" and two other songs.

When his meal was served, Bob returned to the friends and enjoyed the band playing in the background. After dinner, a man approached the table to compliment Bob on his singing. The discussion soon transitioned to racing and to the car they were campaigning at the track.

During the extended discussion, Jack Duffy introduced himself and told Bob he was interested in having someone like him join the Hurst Performance team. He introduced Bob to George Hurst, and Duffy gave Bob his card and invited him to call

Nanci is expecting their second child (daughter Lisa) during the Christmas season with the oldest son, Jim. Their family grew to five with the addition of Jeff a few years later.

him if he wanted to change careers and join the professionals.

A week later, Bob called the number, and Duffy suggested that he call George Hurst's secretary, Gracie, to set up an interview. During the call, he spoke with Jack "Doc" Watson to see if he needed any help on his team. After a few weeks, Bob received a call and was asked to travel to Michigan to interview with Doc and Dave Landrith. Bob drove to Michigan and had a friendly discussion with both Doc and Landrith and was offered a job on the support staff at Hurst.

After accepting the job, Bob was told to meet Paul Phelps the following weekend at a rest stop along the Ohio highway for the next week's races. Paul was an experienced mechanic and fabricator. He was one of the "Hurst Aid" technicians who helped the racers while at the track. Bob's first assignment was alongside Paul as one of these Hurst mechanics to repair the racers' cars that failed tech inspection or broke down on race day.

Bob owned and raced this 1952 Sunbeam Alpine around the time he joined Hurst. The car had a small-block Chevrolet V-8 that replaced the little 4-cylinder engine.

The Alpine was highly customized with the V-8 motor and tilt front end. When Bob wasn't racing this car, he and his brother Dale ran the D&B repair shop in Mansfield, Ohio.

Hurst Performance repaired the racers' cars during the race weekends. The employees who worked on the cars were referred to as Hurst Shifty Doctors. (Photo Courtesy Pete Serio Collection)

The Shifty Doctor name is emblazoned on the side of this Hurst support vehicle. This vehicle has been found and restored and is now owned by collector Joe Spagnoli.

Hurst Hairy Oldsmobile

One of Bob's first assignments at Hurst was to help build a second promotional vehicle. George Hurst's car was a brand-new, front-wheel-drive 1966 Olds Toronado that, according to longtime Hurst employee Don Lane, was immediately fitted with an optional Oldsmobile L69 Tri-Power from a 4-4-2. Knowing the potential of the 455 engine, George decided to build a car with front and rear engines, 455 powered and blown in the lighter 4-4-2 bodystyle. As the crew began construction of this project in the fall of 1965, George searched for a racer who could handle both of the expected 1,000-hp engines. George knew just the man and developed a plan before he called up his friend Joe Schubeck, a former racer and owner of Lakewood Industries in the Cleveland, Ohio, area.

When George called Schubeck and asked to meet him for dinner, he purposely did not disclose his reason for the meeting. Joe had always been impressed with George Hurst and felt that Lakewood Industries was a potential merger candidate with the growing Hurst-Campbell.

Joe met George Hurst, Jack Duffy, and Jack Watson over dinner at the Cleveland airport. George greeted him warmly as "Gentleman Joe" and proceeded to outline his concept of the most outrageous exhibition Funny Car imaginable.

It consisted of a dual-motor, dual-controlled, four-wheel-drive Oldsmobile that featured two gas pedals, a single brake pedal, two shifters, and double everything else. They proceeded to explain the controls and the process needed to accomplish the exhibition. Starting with a front-engine-only burnout, he was then to start the back engine as he was restaging the car at the

The Hurst Hairy Oldsmobile *chassis is finished and painted red. The drivetrain was the next step in the build. Bob Riggle was instrumental in the build of the car.*

Bob was assigned to help build the Hurst Hairy Oldsmobile *when he was not traveling as the mechanic to the* Hemi Under Glass. *Here, a coworker tries to identify the steering wheel configuration during the build.*

The Hurst Hairy Oldsmobile *receives the final prep before the long drive to the Bakersfield debut in 1966.*

The Hurst Hairy Oldsmobile *is shown in its finished form. The rear engine remains hidden other than the conspicuous rear-facing air intake on the back package shelf.*

Christmas tree. He was then to travel the full distance of the quarter-mile in a cloud of smoke generated from the two engines that featured more than 2,000 (combined) horsepower through the four racing slicks.

Joe had a few concerns over the description and realized there was more going on in the cabin than one man could handle. Jack Watson put his fears to rest by describing the new Hurst Line Lock system that hydraulically locked the brakes with a touch of a button that was mounted on the shifter. This freed up both feet so that he could mash the gas pedals to the floor before his launch.

Schubeck had given up driving his Top Fuel dragster the year before to concentrate on his business and explained the time limitations that any new commitment imposed. George told him that Hurst prepared a crew to transport and repair the car and that Joe's only responsibility was to meet them at the track,

The original Hurst Hairy Oldsmobile *was recreated and is now displayed at the Oldsmobile Museum in Lansing, Michigan. (Photo Courtesy Mark Fletcher Collection)*

The Hurst Hairy Oldsmobile *used two blown Oldsmobile 455 engines—each with an estimated 1,000 hp. (Photo Courtesy Mark Fletcher Collection)*

Although many Hurst employees helped construct the car, Dick Chrysler was the traveling mechanic and transport driver for the original Hairy Olds. *(Photo Courtesy Mark Fletcher Collection)*

The Hairy Olds *had two motors, two shifters, two gas pedals, and only one brake. This was a lot for one driver to manage, and the addition of the new Hurst Line Lock product helped the driver to release the front and rear engines simultaneously. (Photo Courtesy Mark Fletcher Collection)*

Miss Hurst Golden Shifter Linda Vaughn poses for a promotional photo. At the track, she would wear an evening gown while driver "Gentleman Joe" Schubeck would wear a top hat and a fire suit that was made to look like a tuxedo. (Photo Courtesy Linda Vaughn Collection)

drive the car, and then fly back to Lakewood to manage his growing business.

George painted the picture a little bit more by showing Gentleman Joe a picture of Linda Vaughn, Miss Hurst Golden Shifter, and described how Joe would wear a fire suit that looked like a tuxedo, complete with a top hat. As Joe climbed into the car, Linda would exchange the top hat and cane for his helmet to send him off in royal style.

The Hurst transport truck carried the **Hairy Oldsmobile**, *repair parts, tires, race fuel, tools, and crew to the major events. Crew members were out for multiple weeks as they crisscrossed the US and attended racing events.*

Fouranado

The car was already in the building process when Bob Riggle joined Hurst and when Joe Schubeck was asked to pilot the rocket initially referred to as either *Fouranado* or *4-4-Two Much*. The car was designed with a full tube frame, which was surrounded by 1966 Oldsmobile 4-4-2 sheet metal. Both engines were attached to twin Turbo 400 automatic transmissions that were combined with two Toronado front-wheel-drive transaxles. The rear-mounted version had the steering components welded into place but retained the independent action and huge disc brakes provided by the front suspension.

To keep the weight bias balanced and provide cooling to the rear engine, John DeJohn of the Hurst team designed the coolant to flow from the front radiator through the tube frame and back. This solution held 33 quarts of coolant that helped disperse the heat created by the combined 2,000 hp of the blown 425-ci mills.

Four identical engines were built for the car by Ray Sissner. Two were installed in the car and two were kept as replacement motors should either or both of the first two fail. The builders of this car included George DeLorean (brother to John DeLorean of Pontiac), Paul Phelps, Ray Sissner, and Bob Riggle.

Bob and Paul were the primary frame builders and utilized all of their talented fabrication and welding skills. In just a few months, the initial concept was designed and created out of raw steel and a pile of high-performance parts. The finished car weighed an impressive 5,800 pounds even with the use of an aluminum hood, trunk, and bumpers. Once completed, the Cutlass was painted in the Hurst traditional black and gold, and Paul Hatton came in to hand-paint the bold graphics on each panel of the car.

The car was introduced to the public at the spring Bakersfield Fuel and Gas meet in California on March 5, 1966. A special ramp truck dubbed the *Hairy Hauler* carried the twin-engined Olds from race to race.

True to George's word, Linda was there to trade out Joe's top hat and cane and send him off in grand style. Joe Schubeck described the first drive as hairy.

"The two major contributing factors were that all this power was being transferred to the four 10-inch racing slicks, causing the car to hydroplane most of the way down the track," Joe said. "This, combined with the intense torque generated by each engine, caused both front wheels to want to walk around the pivot point of the front suspension."

In essence, this caused a severe toe-in condition that created a plowing affect the length of the track that inhibited the ability to steer the car at speed.

At the third race event in Palmdale, California, Joe explained this to his crew chief, Bob "Animal" Lathrum, when a young boy around 12 years old revealed the solution to the experienced racer.

"Why not start with the wheels toed out, so that when you accelerate the wheels go straight?" the boy asked.

Dumbfounded by the simplicity of the solution, this returned control of the car to Joe. The experiment continued until the right mixture of the front-end alignment adjustment was found as well as a series of stronger front steering components.

Hard to Handle

Even with these creative improvements, the car remained a handful to control. Joe was a skilled driver, but early in the season, he slid it into a guardrail during an

The twin-engine four-wheel-drive **Hurst Hairy Oldsmobile** *is almost invisible in the cloud of tire smoke with Joe Schubeck behind the wheel. The open cockpit quickly filled with smoke, which created a dangerous situation when trying to remain straight going down the track.*

Joe Schubeck fills the **Hurst Hairy Oldsmobile** *with smoke at Niagara Raceway in 1967. This picture was taken just before the accident that destroyed the car and caused Joe to retire from driving it. (Photo Courtesy Joe Schubeck Collection)*

event. With all four wheels constantly spinning, the ability to control the car was perilous at best. The car only received superficial damage during this incident and was repaired and repainted in time for the next scheduled race day.

The second and more severe incident happened the following year at Niagara Raceway outside of Buffalo, New York. The car had been freshened to look like the 1967 4-4-2 model. Schubeck did his usual spectacular warm-up presentation. He staged the car at the line with only the front engine running. He performed a smoking burnout with the front motor and noticed that the track was still slick from earlier rain.

Once the car stopped, he started the rear motor and backed to the starting line with both motors running. He staged and set both shifters into drive and set the correlating line-lock buttons to free up both feet from the brake pedal, which he then placed onto the dual gas pedals. He raised the RPM of the two 1,000-hp, nitromethane- and alcohol-fed Oldsmobile engines in unison, released the line locks, shot down the track, and expected to cover the 440 yards in less than 10 seconds and cross the traps at up to 180 mph.

Joe's Out

Approximately 200 yards into this exhibition, with the car engulfed in tire smoke, the front magneto failed and the front engine shut down, turning the barely controllable rocket into the uncontrollable projectile. The *Hurst Hairy Oldsmobile* headed off the track toward the spectators in the bleachers at more than 100 mph.

Joe recalled watching the crowd, which was enthralled over the launch and continued to applaud him as he bared down on the public. He was unable to overpower his momentum with the front engine dead and the slick conditions underfoot. As he passed from the edge of the asphalt, a cable hidden in the standing grass caught the car and redirected it away from the crowd and imminent tragedy.

Joe exited the car with an injured foot and told his crew member Bob "Animal" Lathrum to load it up and take it back to George Hurst and Jack Watson. The car had incurred severe front-end and structural damage from the incident and was never exhibited again. After two years and two serious wrecks, Joe handed in the keys.

Back at the Madison Heights Hurst Performance shop, the car was examined and deemed totaled. Ironically, the same team that helped create the *Hairy Oldsmobile* was charged with dismantling it.

The car was recreated in 2002 by the Hurst Oldsmobile Club of Iowa, utilizing the original hood and aluminum bumpers. The recreated car was built as a representative of the original *Hairy Oldsmobile* but is not a running example because some components were not available, and the car didn't meet the current safety regulations to be run at a sanctioned event. This static replica now resides in the R. E. Olds Transportation Museum in Lansing, Michigan.

Chapter 4

Bob Drives the *Hemi Under Glass*

Bob leans out of the* Hemi Under Glass *for a promotional photo. Bob always made sure to be present at the pits to make sure that the fans were able to see and meet him while driving the* Hemi Under Glass *at events.

When Bob Riggle joined Hurst in the summer of 1965, the first version of the *Hemi Under Glass* had already been built and was entertaining the crowds around the country at drag racing events. Bob was originally assigned to be one of the Hurst Aid mechanics to help racers repair their cars when they broke at the track. This job included basic mechanical repair as well as fabricating and welding aspects.

In addition to helping other racers, Bob occasionally helped Paul Phelps as the mechanic for the *Hemi Under Glass*. Bob was an integral part of the Hurst team and often helped prepare the 1965 *Hemi Under Glass* with Bill Shrewsberry at the wheel.

Although the car had the outward appearance of a stock 1965 Barracuda fastback, the body surrounded a custom full-frame race car. The Chrysler 426 Hemi's horsepower and torque would easily overpower the factory unibody construction, causing it to twist and crumble without the additional strengthening components. The interior flooring was removed, and a new frame was constructed and welded in.

This rear frame assembly supported the increased weight of the Elephant Hemi motor and a marine-application V-Drive assembly, and the rear-end assembly was

confined in a very compact space where the back seat and trunk were located on a production vehicle. The huge rear window allowed the crowds in the pits to get a clear understanding of how all of these components were connected.

Shrewsberry Moves On

Driver Bill Shrewsberry was flamboyant and known to openly boast about his driving talents, suggesting that no one else was capable of handling this "brute

Hurst employee Steve Weiner stands next to the newly finished 1965* Hurst Hemi Under Glass. *This was prior to the first public debut as the car door was not yet adorned with the name of the designated driver Bill Shrewsberry. (Photo Courtesy Steve Weiner)

The finished* Hurst Hemi Under Glass *1965 Barracuda was rolled out of the Madison Heights facility where it was built. Note that there is no driver's name on the top of the door or any sponsor decals.

Bob Riggle and Bill Shrewsberry discuss the* Hemi Under Glass*. Shrewsberry was the driver for the first season with Bob Riggle as his lead mechanic. The second season was the start of Bob Riggle as the driver of the* Hemi Under Glass*, which lasted the next seven decades.

of a ride." Bob explained that Bill was very hard on the Hemi engine's rod and main bearings due to what Bob suspected was over-revving the engine during the performances. Bob chose to test his theory by packing the shifter gates with wheel-bearing grease while they were in Tampa. At the end of a run, Bob asked Bill what gear he hit during the run. Bill stated that he got it into fourth, but Bob checked the gates and found that both third and fourth were still full of grease.

At the end of the first season, Bill had returned from the running at Long Beach, where Riggle was working with Paul Phelps on the *Hairy Olds* at the Hurst plant in Madison Heights. Bob recalled that George called Bill into his office for what was believed to be a renegotiation of the next season's contract.

After 45 minutes, Bill walked out, announced that he was leaving, and asked Riggle to go to Los Angeles as his mechanic for a new wheel-stander, the *L.A. Dart*. Riggle chose to stay with Hurst, and George immediately instructed him to go to Chrysler to pick up 1966 sheet metal to freshen the look of the car to match the current year's production car. Bob ordered a new set of quarter panels, doors, and complete front sheet metal that he grafted onto the 1965 car to transform it into the appearance of the 1966 style.

An Opportunity of a Lifetime

Bob spent the next few weeks working on the *Hairy Olds* alongside Paul Phelps during the day and spent most of his evenings rebuilding the 1965 *Hemi Under Glass* to be current with the 1966 Barracuda styling changes. These changes affected the external fenders and trim of the car and retained the specially built frame and inner body structure including the roofline and the humongous back glass. To accomplish both tasks before the end of the winter break, Riggle set up sleeping quarters in an upstairs office at the Madison Heights building.

Paul Phelps was a good friend with a dramatic sense of humor. Regardless of how late he stayed out the night before, he was always the first to arrive at the Madison

Heights Hurst shop every morning. He entered through the heavy steel door that had a pneumatic spring closure and caused the door to slam shut with a thundering echo throughout the shop. Most people made sure to hold the door from slamming because they knew that Riggle slept in the loft area. Phelps was the exception to the rule and made sure to get the loudest bang possible from the slamming door. He'd burst into laughter when Bob would wake up with a start.

During the reconstruction of the *Hemi Under Glass*, George approached Riggle in March and asked if he felt he could pilot the beast. Although Riggle had traveled with the car and had turned wrenches on it during the season, he had never taken it down the quarter-mile. Not revealing his uncertainty, he convinced George he was capable of piloting the car and added that he could do it without requiring the bottom end of the motor to be rebuilt every weekend.

In early March 1966, Bob found himself at the Detroit Dragway with George Hurst, Leo Kagin, Dave Landrith, Doc Watson, and Jack Duffy to demonstrate his ability to drive the car. With the car prepped and ready to run Bob recalled, "I failed to keep the car straight on the first two attempts and was quickly losing my confidence. So, on the third try, I started in second gear and the car popped right up where I gave George the thumbs up, shifted into third, and walked the car down the track."

On the way back in the other lane, Bob repeated the process to make sure that he impressed the Hurst brass.

Dissecting the Car

As an experienced driver, Bob drove all sorts of race cars and was able to quickly adapt to their unique characteristics. Bob was able to identify the shortcomings of the car and incorporate technical advances into the design of the next version.

Bob developed and built the rear-wheel steering by creating two separate hand controls that slowed down one rear wheel at a time to correct the course as he drove the length of the track with the front wheels up. He refined that capability into the next version with a single handle because he realized that he only needed to steer one way or the other and never both at the same time. Additionally, he never added Positraction to the rear end because it would counteract his ability to steer the car with his individual-wheel braking control.

Get a Grip

While at the 1966 NHRA Spring Nationals at Long Island Dragway, Bob made a launch that popped

Bob Riggle's publicity photo that was taken in the 1966* Hemi Under Glass *that he first piloted for Hurst.

him up onto the rear bumper. The car came back down hard while the rear wheels spun, which shredded the Chrysler 8¾-inch rear end. He promptly replaced it with another Chrysler unit, but eventually Riggle changed to a much stouter GM truck rear end that prevented this from reoccurring.

Smile!

One of the first tasks that Hurst did was take publicity shots of his new driver to be included in newspapers, magazines, and local articles about the *Hemi Under Glass*. Bob was tall, muscular, and handsome. These qualities allowed the Hurst marketing team to play up the change in driving duties to get more attention directed toward Hurst in the automotive press.

Bob was a natural fit as the driver of such a special car. He had a quick wit, liked people, and found them interesting. He always had a big smile and presented an almost movie star persona. Bob was an optimistic person and knew that hard work received positive rewards. Although he had a great Hurst support group involved with the *Hemi Under Glass*, marketing aspects, and fantastic assistance with people like Al Touby, Bob remained a mechanic first and a driver second. He routinely inspected and adjusted the car to make sure it performed as expected for each event.

Bob's Debut

Bob's first appearance at the wheel of the *Hemi Under Glass* was in late March 1966. It was appropriate to be in the Midwest and close to home at US 30 Dragway in Gary, Indiana.

Bob was introduced to the crowd with much fanfare, as the announcer stated that it was about to see something it had most likely never witnessed before. Riggle brought the car to the starting line, opened the door, and climbed out

Drag Cartoon ***magazine featured the 1966*** **Hemi Under Glass** ***on the cover of its June edition. The magazine was geared more for teens and adults rather than young children.***

Bob, with his personalized helmet, stands on a runway before making a run. The open area and smooth surface were ideal for a safe and long wheel-stand.

A young Bob Riggle wears business attire while working with Hurst performance.

to wave to the crowd. He jumped back in, secured his harness, and made a few quick burnouts that caused the car to jump up from the forces. Each time as he backed up to the line, the crowd's excitement increased as the car created a loud and rhythmic *brump, brump, brump* that Bob interrupted with a quick blip of the throttle.

After fully building anticipation from the crowd, he finally staged and hit the throttle to smoothly bring the car up. He ran wheels up about halfway down the course. At the far end, he turned around and drove down the opposing lane back to the starting line. Once there, he lined up for a second pass and allowed the car's pulsating idle to once again invigorate the crowd. On Bob's second trip, he traveled almost to the quarter-mile mark before he let up on the throttle and allowed the front end to drop back down to the tarmac.

Rinse, Repeat . . . Campaigning *Hemi Under Glass*

With the schedule starting to fill for the rest of the 1966 season, Dave Landrith and the marketing team scheduled up to five shows per weekend. Many times, these exhibition runs were in three separate locations with a reasonable driving

Bob Riggle stands next to the original 1966 Barracuda with his mechanic Al Touby. You can see Al's name on the front fender of the car.

distance between them. Bob was and still is a hard worker, and he and his assistant shared the driving duties. They sometimes drove through the night to get to the next day's event.

The weekly routine always began on Monday mornings. This allowed the team time to locate and install any required parts that weren't anticipated. The *Hemi Under Glass* was transported on a Dodge ramp-style, heavy-duty truck. Each Monday, he pulled the car up the ramp so that he could lay

George Hurst sent a memo to Bob Riggle on behalf of a track owner to compliment Riggle on his performance for the spectators. (Photo Courtesy Bob Riggle Collection)

MEMO from GEORGE H. HURST, JR.
PRESIDENT

to Mr. G. H. Hurst DATE 1 June 1966

Mr. Hurst,

Yesterday, May 31, we had a call from Mr. Clark Rader, owner of National Trail Raceways. Mr. Rader said he had never done anything like this before, but he felt compelled to call you and tell you how pleased he was with last Saturday's performance by Bobbie Riggle with the Hemi Under Glass at his Raceway. He said it was the most outstanding performance by a contract runner he had ever seen in his life and the spectators were thrilled. He has had the Little Red Wagon and many others, but none could "hold a candle" to our Hemi and Mr. Riggle. He also said he was very impressed by the mechanic who accompanied Mr. Riggle. "They are two fine boys!"

He feels that the Hemi and Mr. Riggle have made the people in his area Hurst-conscious and increased our prestige.

Mr. Rader had also called Detroit and spoke with Mr. Dave Landreith.

Carol

T.

ccs: Messrs. Campbell, Franzson, Greenwald, Hildebrandt, Palitz and Watson

with the engine over him. The car was designed so that he could easily drop the pan to inspect and replace the main and rod bearings. By doing this procedure each week, only the bearings received wear, and the crank and rods survived for the complete season.

The average week's schedule included traveling either back home to Ohio (if time allowed) or on to the next venue. In the early days, Bob would stay at a hotel close to the track. Most tracks had a place for the teams to plug into shore power and set up a base camp.

Most weeks, they were on site by Thursday evening to be prepared for the Friday night races, when he would try to get in three passes for the crowd. Saturday night was a repeat performance, or, most often, he was at another venue within a few hours' drive. Sunday events were less frequent, and most Sundays were considered a travel day. Come Monday, the process repeated. Bob is proud to say that through diligent maintenance, he never had to cancel an event in his career. Even with systematic maintenance, the unexpected can still happen.

The first year's travel schedule was fairly intense, but Bob was accustomed to it from the previous seasons' work when he was the support staff for the *Hemi Under Glass*. In the spring, they traveled in the South and visited Houston, Atlanta, Memphis, and Mexico City. Then,

Bob "spins out" the 1966* Hemi Under Glass *at the end of his run. He often performed this maneuver to make a second return pass down the track.

Bob Riggle trailered the* Hemi Under Glass *to military hospitals to visit the troops who could not see the car at the races. George Hurst stands on the right side of the photo.

The 1966 **Hemi Under Glass** *sits in front of Bob and his brother Dale's Firebird-brand gas station sign in Mansfield, Ohio.*

When Bob first started with Hurst, the primary manufacturing facility had just been completed in Warminster, Pennsylvania. The new Hurst-Campbell facility allowed for all production to be combined under one roof. Before this, the company had up to 12 different leased production and storage buildings.

they returned north to Indiana to meet with the other Hurst team members for the multiweek Indianapolis 500 events in May.

During the summer months, they went to the Northwest and visited Seattle, San Francisco, Salt Lake City, and drove across the Rocky Mountains to Denver. Then, they crossed over to the Northeast to run at Englishtown, New Jersey, and military-base events near Hurst's home office in Warminster, Pennsylvania. Next, they went back

Riggle launches in Columbus, Ohio, with what appears to be under-inflated tires. Bob learned by reducing the air on the driver-side tire, he could adjust the direction of the car with the motor's torque steer against the extra drag of the lower-pressure tire.

Bob Riggle quickly became an expert at driving the Hemi Under Glass exhibition car. During his first season while racing at Columbus he thrilled the crowd by pulling all four wheels off the ground due to the tremendous horsepower created by the injected Chrysler Hemi engine. (Photo Courtesy Bob Riggle Collection).

toward Columbus, Ohio, and close to his home base of Mansfield, Ohio.

During the winter months, the team headed west to Bakersfield and Pomona after it updated the car at the Ferndale, Michigan, Hurst Performance Center to resemble the newest version of the 1967 Plymouth Barracuda.

Traveling Companions

Al Touby went to school with Nanci in Mansfield. Al met Bob at the Mansfield Porky's burger joint, where the guys with the hot cars often hung out. Bob and Al became friends, and Bob installed a late-model Oldsmobile V-8 in Al's '56 Chevy convertible back in 1960. Through this friendship, Al became a frequent visitor at Bob and Dale's shop in town, which was where the local gearheads gathered to talk after hours. When Bob made it to the *big time* with Hurst, he needed a codriver and assistant to travel with him.

Riggle lifts all four wheels off the ground at Englishtown in 1966. The tracks paid Hurst upwards of $500 per day to entertain the crowds with this wheel-stander. (Photo Courtesy Bob Riggle Collection)

Bob showed up at the construction site for Mansfield's new sewer treatment plant where Al was preparing for a concrete pour by setting rebar. Bob yelled down to Al to ask him if he wanted to travel with him as an assistant to the *Hemi Under Glass*. Al thought about it for a short minute and agreed on the spot to hit the road. Al called down to the foreman from the edge of the pit that he quit and asked him to mail his check.

At the time, Al was newly divorced and had to earn enough to support his three children. Although he was mechanically inclined, he was not on the same level as Bob, who was six years his senior. Initially, Al's responsibilities were to help drive, keep the car clean, and push and prep the car at the tracks. Bob took the role of teacher and mentor and was like a big brother to Al while they traveled. Bob patiently took time to show Al how to pull the Hemi's pan weekly to inspect and replace the bearings. Soon, Al maintained the car to the same level that Bob held himself to as a mechanic.

Bob Riggle and Al Touby (in white T-shirts) prepare the 1966* Hemi Under Glass *before departure from Mansfield, Ohio, for one of the long cross-country journeys.

Over the next two years, Al went everywhere the *Hemi Under Glass* went. They traveled in 48 states (except for Maine and Alaska) and to five Canadian territories. One of the worst continuous trips started in central Ohio, where they drove to Seattle International Raceway in Puyallup, Washington. After they spent one weekend there, they traversed back to an event in Ohio; down to Hialeah, Florida; on to New Orleans; over to Laredo, Texas; down to Mexico City for the Grand Prix; back through Texas; and then home to Mansfield. This four-week trip encompassed 10,000 road miles and countless hotels.

Al was a great traveling companion to Bob, as both had been married and had similar work ethics. The schedule was packed and often required driving through the night after a full evening's performance. Chrysler provided a new 383-powered Plymouth Fury wagon to Hurst as part of the sponsorship of the *Hemi Under Glass*. The Hemi was pulled on an open trailer with the tires and toolbox mounted in the front of the trailer. The two took turns at the wheel, which allowed one person to sleep in the back of the big wagon with the rear seat folded flat while the other drove.

Once they arrived at the track, they checked into a local hotel for the weekend. Most of the racers were friends and tried to stay at the same hotel or in the same general vicinity so they could eat meals and (for many drivers) drink in the bar together. Riggle was not a drinker but joined the others and enjoyed their company. Many times, he was the only one who avoided a hangover the following morning. Often, the Holiday Inn was the hotel of choice—as evidenced by the many embroidered towels that were used in the pits to cover blowers and or permanently soiled by lubricants and grease.

Al only got behind the *Hemi Under Glass* wheel one time. While in Alberta, Canada, the car was pushed in front of the crowd, and Bob convinced Al to put on his fire jacket and helmet. Before he knew it, Al was behind the wheel on the starting line. Bob instructed him in one ear, and the rhythmic sound of the Hemi blasted in the other. Carefully following Bob's direction, Al slowly rolled off the line and then gingerly stabbed the gas, which caused the front wheels to immediately pop up. Without shifting, Al held onto the wheel as the car traveled 60 to 70 feet down the track at about 30 to 40 mph.

Unknowingly, Al's grip on the wheel turned the front wheels toward the open center of the track so that when he let off the gas, the front wheels came down when they weren't straight. The momentum of the car caused it to quickly spin out, doing a 180-degree about-face. He nursed the car back to the starting area, where Bob exchanged the fire jacket and helmet and went on to finish the performance without the crowd or track owner becoming the wiser. Bob admits today that it was both the most thrilling and terrifying day of Al's two years with Hurst.

Unfortunately, the heavy travel schedule became a problem for Al during the first summer, and he chose to return to Mansfield to spend more time with his young family. He was soon back on the road with The Music Explosion, a famous entertainment group from Mansfield. Jack Ehrmantraut jumped at the chance to fill Al's vacancy for the remainder of the season. It was helpful that Jack was also a Mansfield resident because the duo left in the middle of the night on many occasions for the next day's performance.

Dave Landrith booked a lot of the events that first season, and some were as many as 500 miles apart with less than 24 hours to travel. Some weeks, Bob and his traveling companion began with a mid-week Wednesday-night run, Thursday and Friday nights at separate locations, and then a Saturday/Sunday show at the final venue. The Plymouth wagon was turned back into Chrysler with just over 40,000 miles accrued in a little over six months of use. Chrysler disassembled and inspected most of the drivetrain as an analysis of the parts used under the load of towing the heavy trailer and race car.

When the wagon was retired, George Hurst provided a 1966 Pontiac Bonneville two-door hardtop as the tow car. Bob remembered that although it had the 389 V-8 engine, it had more than enough power for towing. He also recalled that the backseat was a bit cramped for his tall frame and therefore it wasn't as comfortable as the long Plymouth wagon.

After the short-lived *Hurst Hairy Olds* season of 1966, the *Hairy Olds* was retired and the Ford F-700 tilt cab hauler (referred to as the *Hairy Hauler*) was offered to Riggle to haul the *Hemi Under Glass*. This system had the additional sleeper bunk behind the seats, which allowed the drivers to take shifts and catch a few hours of sleep as they traveled. Occasionally, Paul Phelps took Al Touby's place and joined as Bob's traveling assistant and mechanic on some of these trips.

Bringing the Family

Bob was an active father of three and returned home as often as possible. When he had exhibition runs close to his hometown of Mansfield, he often brought along one of the young boys or the whole family to participate. During these early years as the driver of the *Hemi Under Glass*, the trips away from home were long, and free time with the family was highly valued.

Over the years, his involvement with the Firebird gas station and the shop he ran in partnership with his brother Dale became less frequent.

Bob Riggle rarely returned to the family's Mansfield, Ohio, service station due to his busy schedule. While there between appearances, he took this photo of the* Hemi Under Glass. *(Photo Courtesy Bob Riggle Collection)

The big Chrysler Hemi engine fills the backseat area and is visible under the oversized rear window of the 1967 Barracuda.

The original 1967 Hemi Under Glass *would rub the rear bumper when it first jumped up to the wheelie. In some instances, the rear wheels completely lifted off the ground. Bob soon added a wheelie bar to make the takeoffs more controllable.*

He eventually sold the gas station and relinquished the reins of the brothers' shared business into Dale's sole control.

Regardless of the personal toll, the heavy travel schedule, and the job challenges that Bob and his family faced, he truly enjoyed driving the *Hemi Under Glass* and constantly looked for ways to improve the entertainment value of his performances while helping the track owners grow their attendance numbers whenever the *Hemi Under Glass* was on the schedule. Because of his loyalty and willingness to go the extra mile for the owners and their fans, the track owners who began as customers became close friends to Bob and most of the Hurst team.

Many of these friendships continued over multiple decades as the tracks either continued to prosper or were forced out due to the encroachment of new developments into the rural farmlands that once hosted these active drag strips. There are no active tracks in the United States that Bob can't tell you the history of the owners and most details about multiple generations of the families who operated them.

Wheel-Standing on Ovals

Although the *Hemi Under Glass* was normally run on a flat drag strip, Bob was asked to perform for the NASCAR crowd in North Carolina in 1966. He explained that he was able to get the Barracuda to pop up on the angled track, but it wanted to turn right and started climbing the track as he went in front of the grandstands.

"I was able to gently bring the car back down and go around Turns 1 and 2 where I crowded to the lower part of the track and popped a wheelie the full length of the back straight, bringing the front wheels down in just enough time to bring the car through Turn 3 at speed, NASCAR style," Bob said.

Normally, the NASCAR crowd and the drag racing crowd were two different types of fans. However, Bob was pleasantly surprised by the appreciation of those in attendance.

"When the race was over, I was with the car in the pits and was swarmed by the enthusiastic crowd," he said.

Hawaii Visit

George Hurst was a veteran who finished his naval career at the Johnsville Base in Warminster, Pennsylvania, which is the same town where he launched his Hurst-Campbell business just a few years later.

As the Hurst company grew, George always looked for new opportunities to give back to the hardworking servicemen and servicewomen. One way that Hurst assisted was by creating a monthly racing industry newsletter titled "The Defenders: The Hurst Armed Forces Club" and delivering this quarterly newsletter to soldiers in Vietnam. The idea was to ship copies to the oversea bases so that the service personnel could follow motorsports happenings in the United States. This also helped extend Hurst's reach to potential future customers and helped those serving in the armed forces to feel connected with motorsports back home.

Additionally, Hurst worked with all branches of the armed forces to entertain the troops at special events. An exciting exhibition car

Bob made sure to interact with the young crowd that came out to see the* Hemi Under Glass *at military bases. He is shown preparing to make a run for the young soldiers and their families.

The 1966* Hemi Under Glass *entertains the naval personnel at the base located just a few miles from the Hurst production facility in Warminster, Pennsylvania.

Bob Riggle often performed for the servicemen. Here, he is at the Jonestown naval base in Warminster, Pennsylvania.

like the *Hemi Under Glass* was the perfect vehicle to entertain the platoons. It was a self-contained show even when not performing at a sanctioned drag race event.

The obvious location to boost morale was in Hawaii because most Vietnam-bound troops both mustered and returned through multiple bases located there. The first event in Hawaii took place in the spring of 1966. The newly refinished 1966 *Hurst Hemi Under Glass* weighed just over 3,400 pounds and was loaded onto a United Airlines cargo plane in Los Angeles, California. Hurst/Campbell paid for all the costs. The Hurst team consisted of Bob Riggle, Dick Chrysler, Jack Watson, Linda Vaughn, and George Hurst, and all traveled with the *Hemi Under Glass* to three Hawaii military bases to entertain more than 60,000 troops, including visits to those confined to military hospitals.

The typical spring weather was overcast and wet for most of the 1966 trip. The *Hemi Under Glass* was scheduled to run at the Wheeler Air Force base, but there was torrential rain that day. Bob knew he'd have trouble maintaining enough equal rear-wheel traction to safely bring the car up straight.

The decision was made to move the large crowd into the flight hanger with the end doors opened. The hanger measured 400 feet, which was longer than a football field and adequate for a safe run. The crews hurriedly moved the aircraft from

George Hurst was a veteran of the US Navy and made sure that the soldiers who defended our country were treated to special events for the military. It was common for the Hurst team to visit many US bases to entertain and interact with those who were enlisted.

To take the **Hemi Under Glass** *overseas, it had to be loaded on a plane for the flight. United Airlines sponsored the shipping of the car to Hawaii so that Hurst could perform at the multiple military bases in the state.*

the center of the hanger while Bob prepped the car.

Bob was staged just inside the door where the concrete was dry, and he was able to easily bring up the car and drive on two wheels between the crowd and the million-dollar military jets on each side. As he exited out the back door, he came down on the concrete pad that extended to the runway. Unbeknownst to Bob, the surface was covered in jet fuel and rain, which caused the *Hemi Under Glass* to spin out (a full 360 degrees). For the young fliers and their families, Bob put on a very memorable show.

When the team continued its journey with a visit to the Tripler Medical Hospital, where many servicemen who had been severely wounded in Vietnam were recuperating. Many faced a long road to recovery before they were sent home.

Linda Vaughn entered the hospital and encouraged the injured to get up and move outside to see the show. Many were seated in chairs or wheelchairs, using crutches, or in hospital beds that were rolled out so the wounded could be propped up and participate in the event. Other soldiers assisted by carrying out those who were not mobile enough to make it on their own.

Although they were not able to run the *Hemi Under Glass* on the hospital grounds, most of the enlisted soldiers were able to get their picture taken with Bob and Linda, and they got to see and hear the Hemi engine roar to life.

Between the scheduled events, the Hurst team enjoyed some sightseeing. While on the island, Bob and Nanci attempted to teach Linda how to water ski on one of the lakes, which she successfully accomplished. Additionally, the Hurst team enjoyed riding motor scooters around Hawaii and even rode them

Riggle spun out the car at the end of the track to line up and perform a second run. You can see the passenger rear slick is rolling under and dangerously close to losing air pressure at the bead of the wheel.

Linda Vaughn, Bob Riggle, and George Hurst stand among the US military personnel in Hawaii. Some of the individuals were released from the hospital so that they could attend the show and meet the Hurst employees.

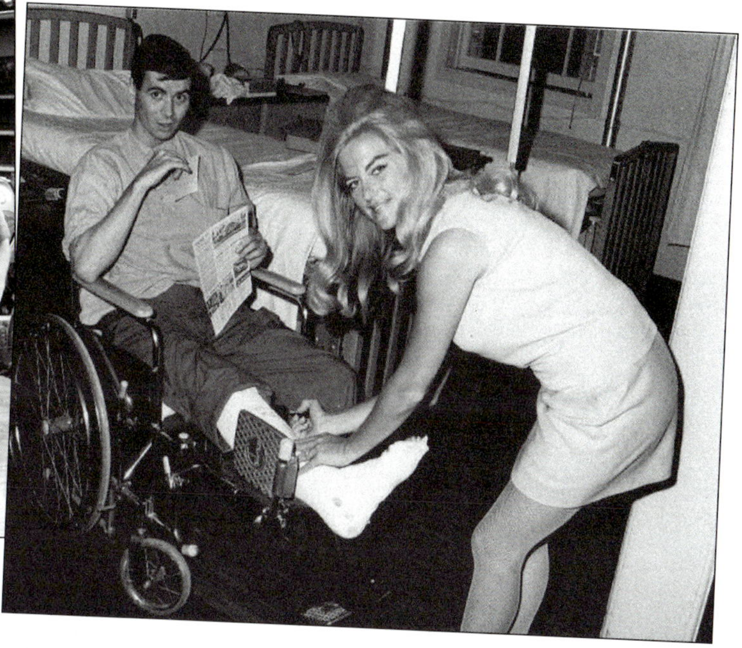

Linda takes time to sign the cast of an enlisted man who couldn't leave the hospital. He is holding a copy of the **Hurst Defenders** *magazine that Hurst published and distributed at the bases.*

HURST DEFENDERS ARMED FORCES CLUB

PERFORMANCE REPORT

VOL. 2 NO. 10 HURST ARMED FORCES CLUB OCTOBER, 1967

SUPER STOCKS HEAD FOR TULSA

NHRA WORLD POINTS FINALS

● TULSA, Okla. -- First there were 43, then there were 16 ... 8 ... 4 ... 2 ... and finally one big winner. Sound confusing -- well it might be to some, but to the 43 Super Stock [illegible] journeying to Tulsa, Oklahoma for the NHRA World Points Finals, Oct. 28-29, this "numbers game" is a pure quarter-mile of gold.

Still mixed up? Here's what it's all about. The NHRA World Championship Series has qualified 43 Super Stock racers for the World Finals in Tulsa, not to mention a host of the country's quickest AA/Fuelers, gas rails, comp machines and stocks in the other eliminators. Top Fuel and the various eliminators are in for their share of the spotlight at the World Finals, but the biggest share of the glory is being reserved for the Super Stock contestants.

The seven division champs are guaranteed a starting line spot in the finals and qualifying will produce another nine cars out of the 43 to make up a 16 car field. Still we're just talking about another group of late-model stockers at another drag race. Well, this is a super-special field of drivers and cars who will be battling it out for the World Champion title. And therein lies the story.

Super Stocks are "what's happenin." Late 1966 was about the time those 'funny cars' started to become a little un-funny. Those one-piece fiberglass bodied creations started reaching into the 170 mph range, lowering elapsed times and seemingly at the same time, their accident rate went up.

Most of the leading drivers have had their share of close calls in these cars with several lives being lost in recent months. After several close calls and a quick glance of the potentially dangerous situation, such names as Hubert Platt, Sox & Martin, and Dick Landy exchanged their funny car ride for a brand new factory-fresh super stocker.

They've been over-shadowed in the awards department by the fuelers and funny cars. Not anymore! George Hurst decided to focus the spotlight on the stock cars by awarding $10,000 to the '67 World Super Stock Champ. Hurst made this bombshell announcement at the '66 Finals in Tulsa to give the little guy of racing - the stocker - more consideration and attention. Now they have a chance for a big payday. Other supporters and equipment manufacturers jumped on the bandwagon and the project has snowballed in the '67 drag season with super stocks receiving the lions' share of crowd response. (Continued on Page 2)

1

The **Hurst Defenders** *magazine was designed and published by Hurst for the servicemen around the world. Hurst hosted an Armed Forces Club where the servicemen enrolled and received the flyer in the mail at no cost.*

Five young men are wearing their hospital clothes and slippers while getting signatures from Bob Riggle and the beautiful Linda Vaughn while inspecting the **Hemi Under Glass.**

along the shore out by some of the blowholes.

Linda recreated the trip to Hawaii in 1968 and visited the patients at Hickman Air Base hospital. She represented Hurst along with the "Drag-On Lady" Shirley Shahan and racer Hayden Proffitt on an American Motors–sponsored trip.

First Mexico Trip in 1966

The *Hemi Under Glass* was invited to travel to Mexico City in the spring of 1966 to do an exhibition at a drag race and then be shown to the public at the World of Wheels event. This was a paid event where the host track paid Hurst a fee and offered to cover the travel expenses of Bob and the Hurst team to attend.

Paul Phelps, Al Touby, and Bob drove down to Mexico and towed the *Hemi Under Glass* on an open car hauler. George Hurst and his wife, along with Linda Vaughn, flew to Mexico City and met with the team there. Bob and Paul left Ohio and took turns driving the grueling 2,200 miles to Mexico City. The plan included crossing the border into Mexico at Laredo, Texas.

As the team drove into Mexico City, the organizer arranged for them to be met by the police chief on a motorcycle at a truck stop outside of the city. The police chief escorted the Hurst crew to the hotel for the night and to the track the next day.

Because of their shared love of motorcycles, Bob and the chief became fast friends and drinking buddies. It turns out the police chief was also the top man on the police motorcycle acrobatics exhibition team. The acrobatics team created a human pyramid of up to 17 police officers perched on four moving motorcycles for local parades and at the Mexico City race track. The motorcycles circled the track side by side with the different officers staged around the track who ran and climbed aboard the moving platform until the police chief was the final man to adorn the top of the pyramid.

When they arrived at the track, the *Hemi Under Glass* was secluded in a small garage next to the track while they performed their prerun checklist. When it was time for his exhibition run, Bob climbed into the Barracuda and was quickly surrounded by the crowd as he pulled into his staging lane. Bob was concerned with safety, and he felt the lack of crowd control was too dangerous for him to attempt the run, so he called over his new friend (the chief of police) and asked for a little help. The motorcycle brigade soon moved the crowd back to the fence line and allowed Bob to safely make his exhibition runs both up and back down the track in front of a very enthusiastic crowd.

After the run, Bob brought out the two minibikes that Hurst used as transportation around the track and challenged the chief to race around the track. Bob made sure that the police chief crossed the finish line first in front of the large crowd.

Later, when the team was relaxing back at the hotel, the chief pulled up, and Bob asked to drive the police-specification Harley-Davidson motorcycle around the hotel property. Bob drove around the block instead, which caused the chief to fear for Bob's health because if one of his officers saw Bob on his motorcycle, there was a chance that Bob might return injured or at least with a few anxious officers in hot pursuit.

Second Mexico Trip: (Shirley Shahan's Thoughts) October 23, 1966

Later that year, Hurst was again invited to attend the Mexico City Grand Prix event. Bob Riggle and race driver Shirley Shahan had become good friends over the summer racing season in 1966, so when

Shirley Shahan and her husband, H. L. Shahan, traveled with Bob Riggle and others through Mexico for the Mexico City Grand Prix event. (Photo Courtesy Shirley Shahan Collection)

Bob was invited to visit Mexico City again in the fall, he invited Shirley and her husband H. L. to bring their 1965 Plymouth Belvedere that had a 426 Hemi and an automatic. Shirley was a fierce competitor under the "Drag-On-Lady" moniker and was about to set a new record as the first female to win at the NHRA Winternationals as Top Stock Driver. Shirley did the driving, and H. L. was the mechanic. Plymouth supplied the car and parts, which allowed the team to dominate the SS/BA division on the West Coast and beyond.

The plan was for Shirley, H. L., and one of her young crew members named George to meet with Bob, Nanci, Al Touby, and the other racers in Laredo, Texas, where they would cross the border and caravan for two days and drive 700 miles directly south to Mexico City. The group also included Don Gay and his brother Carl, who raced a red altered-wheelbase 1965 Pontiac GTO out of Houston, Texas; racer Mike Brown with his red Hemi Dodge; racer Doug Thorley and his wife, Betty; and *Hot Rod* magazine's Ray Brock.

The group was delayed most of the day at the border in Laredo as Ray Brock, who organized the group, did not have the correct paperwork to allow the race cars and tow rigs into Mexico and guarantee their return across the US border one week later.

After many hours of discussions and the preparation of new paperwork, the team was allowed into Mexico. It was late afternoon and they planned to stay overnight in the little town of Saltillo, Mexico, that evening.

Although Saltillo was only 200 miles from Laredo, the path went through many small villages on barely paved roads. When conditions allowed, Riggle led the caravan at speeds over 90 mph with the open-trailered race cars bouncing around on the rough roads behind them. As night fell, they discovered that the locals drove this two-lane road with their lights off and only turned them on when they identified any oncoming traffic. After a few close calls, the caravan became somewhat accustomed to the practice. There were many occurrences when the lead car thought they were alone on the highway only to have a car surprisingly turn on its lights at the last minute and forced the driver to dive to the right edge of the road with a string of cars and trailers fishtailing behind.

They arrived at the beautiful hotel in Saltillo late in the night, tired, and hungry. As they prepared for bed, the women discovered wires hidden behind each mirror in the rooms. They determined that the wires connected some type of camera system, and they draped their coats over the mirrors before turning in for the night.

The following day's journey was in the daylight and therefore less eventful. Shirley recalled that once they arrived in Mexico City, they were escorted through the town for safety reasons. That part worked out well except for when they stopped for some sightseeing and Don Gay's brother Carl was mugged on the first night and lost all of his money.

The next day was the race and show. Shirley was doing a burnout in preparation for a run and was shocked to find out that dozens of spectators were allowed to come right up to touch the car in the process. After H. L. insisted that the crowd be moved back, the racers safely performed their match races and made sure that each driver had his or her fair share of wins.

Between the match racing events performed by the racers, Bob performed with the *Hemi Under Glass* for the full length of the racetrack. He recalled that crowd control was nonexistent with civilians along the track almost for the full distance of the course.

Shirley said that once they crossed the border into the United States at Laredo, each race team went its separate way in relative safety. George was driving the two-lane Highway 90 between Marfa and Van Horn, Texas, when his trailer lost a wheel at around 70 mph. Shirley remembered looking back over her shoulder and being able to read the lettering on the side of her car as it was jackknifing behind the tow wagon. They stopped safely and found the missing wheel in the ditch. They carefully removed the Hemi Plymouth from the trailer and dragged the trailer to the next small town, where the broken axle was welded back together. It required one more stop along the road home to have the axle repaired more permanently.

Bob's Recollections

On the second trip, arrangements were made to meet at a large truck stop outside of town where they met with a police escort for the final portion of the trip into Mexico City. Because the city was preparing for the Mexico City Grand Prix, the officers never arrived to lead the team downtown.

Bob became impatient and decided he could navigate the caravan to the host hotel. Within a few miles, a local police officer on a motorcycle pulled them over and refused to allow them to continue.

Bob was familiar with the system and produced a $20 bill to the officer, who promptly included another officer in a 1958 Chevy to help the caravan get to the hotel.

The next day at the event, Bob ran into the police chief whom he had earlier befriended. When the chief asked him how he made it through town alone, Bob mentioned that he received an escort but that he paid a fee for the service. The chief was infuriated and quickly drove off on his motorcycle. He returned a short time later with a patrol car and other officers. The motorcycle officer from the previous day was with the chief and humbly apologized to Bob and returned the $20. The chief dressed down the officer and removed the badge from his uniform. Bob was concerned about the health of the officer and asked the chief what would happen to him. The chief told Bob that no harm would come to him but that the officer needed to find a new profession.

Hemi Under Glass!

The *Hemi Under Glass* caused some emotional responses for the audience. One time, while in the pits in Salem, Ohio, a man came running toward Bob yelling, "*Hemi Under Glass, Hemi Under Glass*!" The man's wife pleaded with Bob to allow her husband to sit in the car, which Bob was happy to oblige. It turned out that the man knew the *Hemi Under Glass* from photos in car magazines that he read while he was in Vietnam.

As he sat in the car, the young veteran began to cry and explained that it had been a dream for him to see the car in person, and now that he was sitting in the seat with his own hands on the wheel, he realized life could return to normal.

When the Hurst team traveled around the United States to visit the military bases, it often brought the oversized shifter that was designed to rest on a platform on the trunk of one of the cars. Here, the servicemen help install the platform so that Linda Vaughn can stand with the shifter for the event.

Linda Vaughn is waiting at the races to do a parade lap standing on the platform with the giant Golden Hurst shifter.

This is one of many stories that remind Bob and his wife, Nanci, that the *Hemi Under Glass* was more than an exhibition car. During a time of unrest and international conflicts, it became a unique reflection of an American lifestyle and served to vanquish the relentless hunger for everything fast and loud.

1967: A New Year and a New Car

The Barracuda design was drastically changed for the 1967 model year. Although the Barracuda fastback still had an expansive rear window area, it was no longer wrapped around the sides of the rear quarter panels. For this reason, the Hurst team chose to start from scratch for the 1967 year. Chrysler soon delivered two body-in-white packages to the Hurst facility in Ferndale, Michigan.

The reason for the two bodies was to build a backup car in case the *Hemi Under Glass* was damaged in some way. The backup car was never

Riggle is performing a nighttime run in the original 1967 Barracuda with the short skid/spark plates attached right below the bumper. Always the ham, he looks directly at the camera as he flies by.

The 1966 car was set aside when Bob Riggle built a new version of the* Hemi Under Glass *for 1967. The drivetrain was reused for this body change.

The new 1967 Barracuda was built at the Ferndale, Michigan, Hurst performance building. The headlights were trailer hubcaps mounted where the headlights occupied the grille.

put to use and remained in storage at the Hurst Performance building in Madison Heights. Over the years, Bob tried to find out what happened to the spare car, but it seems to have simply disappeared. If anyone knows as to where it might be, please let Bob Riggle know.

Chrysler remained a major sponsor for the *Hemi Under Glass*. Bob was offered a new 1-ton Dodge cab and chassis from Chrysler at no cost. He accepted the generous offer and built a car hauler ramp with a toolbox and storage underneath. The truck was painted black, and Bob painted the custom-built ramp and boxes a contrasting bright white. This truck proved to be ultra-dependable and remained with Bob as long as he campaigned the Barracuda-bodied cars.

The car was booked solid for the 1967 race season, and any delay for body repairs caused a cancellation to the schedule. By this time, many other wheel-standers were on the market, and many of the engagements were match races between two or more of the friendly competitors.

Kids Loved Bob

While camping at the Stanton track, Bob had a quad that he used as the push car for the *Hurst Hemi Under Glass*. He could pop a wheelie with it and started playing on the track with titanium pucks attached to the back rack. Some of the kids saw him doing this, and Jim thought that it would be great if Bob performed a special run for the kids on it during the Friday night event. He felt that the kids could identify with the quad more than the *Hemi Under Glass* because most of the kids rode dirt bikes or quads themselves. Bob did a short but successful display and was swamped by the kids in the pits after the run.

When Bob performed at 75/80 raceway in Maryland, he looked over the fence and saw a 10-year-old boy frantically waving at him. Bob walked over, lifted him over the fence, and let him sit in the Barracuda. He then walked around the car and explained the different controls to him. He signed a poster for the boy and then returned him over the fence to his parents. That same boy wrote Bob a letter in 2019 and

Hand-Control Sticks

The 1967 Plymouth Barracuda went through a major upgrade to a larger platform. To represent the current model year, Bob Riggle built a whole new car and transferred the drivetrain components into the new body.

By 1967, the Hemi Under Glass *was well known and drew large crowds whenever it appeared. Bob installed a passenger seat so that he could give rides to brave and daring passengers.*

The new build allowed Bob to make additional changes to the *Hemi Under Glass* design. For the first two years, the car could not steer while the front two wheels were carried down the track. Bob learned how to use the throttle and the torque of the supercharged Hemi to continuously correct direction ever so slightly to try and keep in his lane. This was effective for the showmanship side of the *Hemi Under Glass* but made it difficult to keep in the gas when up against one of the match race wheel-standers. Bob's solution was to create a hand-brake control that allowed him to independently apply drag to either rear wheel once in the air and cause the car to turn in that direction. Initially, this was designed with two-hand-control sticks, one for each rear wheel.

Bob found that he was constantly moving back and forth between the two controls and realized he could combine them into one. When he pushed the stick forward, it applied the left brake and turn the car to the left. If he pulled back, it applied the right rear brake and caused the car to go right. Bob explained that on windy days, he wore the stick out with its continuous forward and rear motion, which caused the car to walk on two wheels going down the track.

One additional major change for the 1967 year was the switch from the 4-speed manual to the TorqueFlite automatic transmission, which was still controlled by a Hurst shifter. The big advantage to this change was that it allowed Bob to have a free hand to adjust direction using the hand-brake stick or to wave to the crowd as the *Hemi Under Glass* flew by.

One week while performing in Salt Lake City on a Friday night, the transmission failed. Bob and Nanci loaded the injured car onto the trailer and drove through the night to Bandimere Speedway in Denver where he replaced the transmission with his spare unit on Saturday morning and ran the car that afternoon. The next event was two weeks later at the same location, so the track owner allowed Bob and Nanci to stay in the motor home at the Bandimere facility.

During those two weeks, Nanci and Bob explored Pikes Peak, Colorado Springs, and the Garden of the Gods like regular tourists. Bob also picked up the necessary transmission parts so that he had a spare in case of failure. After two weeks, the *Hemi Under Glass* was once again featured at an event along with a couple of thundering jet cars. Nanci loved the power and sound of the jet cars. Even with all the excitement surrounding this overwhelming display of raw power, the crowd stood on its feet when the *Hemi Under Glass* was introduced and made Bob feel like he was a true celebrity.

The track in Stanton, Michigan, was an impressive 4,000 feet long. Bob and Nanci showed up a few days early for an event and were allowed to camp in the motor home on the track property. The owner, Jim, was having issues with power for the overhead lights and asked Bob to help by checking the circuits. Jim killed the power and Bob started checking each ground on the circuits. He quickly found one wiring end that was showing signs of being burnt. Bob cleaned up the wire end and the connector and reconnected it. When Jim threw the master switch, all the lights and the starting tree worked.

Bob shared this as an example of why he performed preventative maintenance on his race cars. Ignoring a simple issue could turn into a major disaster in front of a full grandstand.

The 426 Hemi bakes under the Arizona sun at Beeline in 1967. (Photo Courtesy Wes Eisenschenk)

Bob makes sure to touch the pads to the pavement, sending sparks behind the original 1967 car as it exhibits for the crowds at Beeline Raceway in Mesa, Arizona.

told him how the incident inspired him to be a race car mechanic. At 62 years old, he thought that it was time to let Bob know what that chance interaction had meant to him.

Big Daddy at Beeline

Some of the events were more memorable than others for a different reason. When the wheel-standers were invited to attend a special event, they were normally paid a negotiated fee by the track owner on the last night from the gate receipts.

In 1967, Don Garlits put on a big American Hot Rod Association event at the Mesa, Arizona, Beeline Raceway with a large list of wheel-standers. The track owner collected the gate receipts, and when it was time for each of the wheel-standing drivers to get paid, the owner had absentmindedly left the track with the gate receipts. "Big Daddy" Don Garlits had to track him down so that everyone could get paid before they hit the road.

Pappy Hart ran Lions Drag Strip in Long Beach, California. One evening at a special wheel-stander event, he set up a competition to see who could stay aloft for the longest distance down the track. Bill "Maverick" Golden ran the *Little Red Wagon* down the track, and then Pappy Hart dropped a burning flare where he landed to mark the distance for the other drivers to surpass. Next was Chuck Poole with the *Chuck Wagon*, who ran and tried to beat him bypassing the flare.

On the second run, Maverick went almost to the end of the track. When he came down, he told Pappy Hart to not drop the flair for fear that Chuck would not have enough track to stop after passing it.

It was a great plan, but everyone forgot to inform Chuck that there was no flare to surpass. Chuck took off as the evening fog rolled in off the water and shrouded the far end of the track. By the time Chuck realized there was no flare to pass, it was too late, and he was in the air when he ran out of pavement. There were huge metal gas lines at the end of the track. Chuck intentionally spun out the Dodge A-100 at the last second, which sacrificed the truck but saved his life.

The *Chuck Wagon* was rebuilt by Sherman Gun and Mike Hoage, who used a Volkswagen pickup cab with fold-down sides. The original drivetrain was salvageable, and the *Chuck Wagon* had a new look while retaining the familiar Hemi engine in the back.

Earlier, Bob had jumped into the bed of Holly Swindle's backup pickup and was almost bumped out during a hard landing. The truck was later sold to George Tours, and Bob was allowed to drive the truck at the Irwindale Raceway.

The different handling characteristics, as compared to the *Hemi Under Glass*, became immediately obvious. When the *Hemi Under Glass* went airborne, the driver sat ahead of the motor and went up with the front end. However, because of the reverse configuration of the backup pickup, Bob pulled the wheelie and was somewhat surprised that he went down as the back of the truck and the motor went up in front of him. Regardless of the difference, Bob kept the front (or back) aloft both down and on the return side of the track.

Sky Racing

On more than one occasion, Bob was involved in a promotion that involved him racing an airplane. The first time was in Kingman, Arizona, and the stunt pilot was a dentist from Las Vegas. Driving the original 1967 car, the idea was to have the two stunt vehicles cross the midsection of the airport at the same time. Bob was staged at the far end of the runway. A truck at the other end of the track flashed his headlights to let Bob know the plane was approaching him from behind.

On the first run, the plane was too early. For the second attempt, Bob started earlier and was going down the track in high gear with the nose of the car at full elevation as the plane caught up and flew over inverted with a smoke trail. A fantastic photo was taken of the two vehicles at speed.

Bob also had a similar run with a US Navy Blue Angels aircraft, except the jet plane flew inverted over the top of the *Hemi Under Glass* and the pilot gave Bob a thumbs up (or down) as he flew over. The cockpit of the airplane was so close that Bob felt he could reach out and shake hands with the pilot.

Connie Swingle was from Oklahoma and ran the Corvair *Teleflex* that was later called the *Trash Truck*. During one race that Bob attended with him, Connie lost control, left the track, and hit a telephone pole right in the center of the flat front-end pickup, which drove the steering column into his crotch. Luckily, he was not hurt in the incident.

Another time, Connie broke a rod on the 427 big-block Chevrolet engine when he was at the track. Like many of the part-time drivers, he drove the truck to the track from his shop and did not have a tow

Bob races a stunt plane at the Kingman, Arizona, airport. The idea was for Bob and the plane to cross the finish line at the same time. The plane's speed made this nearly impossible to time, although they made multiple attempts.

Connie Swingle drove for Don Garlits before campaigning his own mount,* Trash Truck. *Once after making a pass at Irwindale and heading back to the pits on the return road, Swingle saw Riggle powering down the track, so he too hit the gas and both wheel-standers flew by each other in the opposite direction. (Photo Courtesy John Olcott)

vehicle for the 60-mile trip home. He removed the pan, extracted the broken rod, cut it down to the round portion, and reinstalled it to maintain oil pressure while he drove home on only seven cylinders.

The track owners were always pretty good promoters. At one event that the *Hemi Under Glass* and *L.A. Dart* both attended, the announcer witnessed how close the Barracuda was to the banner that was strung across both lanes of the track about 100 feet from the starting line. He convinced Riggle and Shrewsberry to make multiple attempts to see if they could catch the front bumper and pull down the banner. They came close, but neither one succeeded. Riggle was declared the winner for coming closer than the *L.A. Dart*. At a later date, Bob caught a banner strung across the Norwalk, Ohio, track with the 1967 car even though he didn't compete at that event.

The wheel-standers and the drag racers shared a camaraderie on the road. Sometimes this friendship led to a few practical jokes. Bob Riggle realized that the *L.A. Dart* was designed so that it easily transferred the weight off the front to the rear wheels when it didn't have the weight of a driver in the car. He found four 1-gallon water jugs and stashed them in the open trunk area above the rear bumper. With the additional weight added to the back, he could lean on the car and cause the front wheels to lift off the ground.

The First Wreck at Irwindale

The Irwindale track in Southern California was one of the closest raceways to Los Angeles and a popular location for the wheel-standers to perform. During one of these events in 1967, Bob had a successful run down the track and spun the car at the far end by the big tree. He then came back down in the left lane and did a second wheel-stand back to the pits.

On this day, Bob spun the car around, and just as it started facing correctly in the lane, the front wheels popped up and Bob navigated the *Hemi Under Glass* in the air on the quarter-mile back toward the pits. He approached the starting line in front of the stands and gently brought the car down. Bob was unaware that the front wheels were still turned left from the turn

Bob made a contest of attempting to pull down the banner that was normally above the starting line. By backing up and starting in the burnout box, the front edge of the hood came extremely close to touching the banner.

Late 1960s stylized paint was a sign of the times. The paint job did not have enough black to satisfy George Hurst. Hurst was known for the contrasting black and gold paint schemes on all of its company cars that were present at the various sponsored racing events. (Photo Courtesy Ted Pappacena/dragracingimagery.com)

around on the far end of the track. The car immediately darted left, the left front fender hit the right-lane guardrail, the back of the car spun around counterclockwise, and the right rear tire jumped over the guardrail.

The motor was still revving, and the car jumped back over the rail and landed upright on the track. Bob was able to drive the car back to the pits where he discovered that the left front fender was damaged and the metal down the full right side of the car was gouged. Luckily, no one was injured, and there was no structural damage to the car.

1968

For 1968, the 1967 primary car was refreshed with a new grille and taillight trim. Through each version, Bob continued to use full steel body panels. The agreement with Chrysler was that it supplied the needed body parts because it was important to Chrysler that the car reflected the current Barracuda model that was available to the public.

Bob chose to get creative with the paint scheme for 1968 and created a design with a large Hurst shifter image on each side of the car. This was a drastic change from the traditional gold with black trim that the public had seen over the last three years. George Hurst saw the new paint job just before the *Hemi Under Glass* trip to the Puerto Rico event and requested that Bob repaint the car when they returned stateside.

The Hurst Company went through some major changes in the second half of 1968. By the summer of 1968, both Bill Campbell and Jack "Doc" Watson had departed Hurst for new endeavors. The company transitioned from being privately held to being publicly held. With this dramatic change came a huge influx of cash to the four company partners.

When the new Sunbeam executives went to a *Hemi Under Glass* exhibition, they decided that the potential liability was not in the

When Bob updated the 1967 car to 1968 trim, he painted it in a more hip and striking color combination. When George Hurst saw it, he requested it be repainted in the traditional black and gold colors. (Photo Courtesy Bill McDonnell Sr. Collection)

One paint job that Riggle experimented with had a giant Hurst shifter painted on the side of the car. Although many liked it, George Hurst did not. Therefore, the combination was short-lived.

Riggle leaves the line at New York National Dragway in 1968. The heavy Hurst mags had been replaced by lighter magnesium gray spoked wheels. (Photo Courtesy Ted Pappacena/dragracingimagery.com)

best interest of the corporation. Jack Duffy created an agreement where Bob Riggle was able to purchase the *Hurst Hemi Under Glass* over one year. Sixty percent of the event proceeds went to Bob as the new owner, and 40 percent were put into an account that applied to pay the company for the *Hemi Under Glass* car, ramp truck, and marketing franchise.

After the agreed-upon one-year period, Jack Duffy sent a letter to Bob that gave him full ownership of the *Hemi Under Glass* franchise. As the new owner of the *Hemi Under Glass*, Bob repainted the Barracuda gold with psychedelic green sides, spider webs, and large chrome letters.

The Hemi Under Glass *at full height allows you to see the two skid pads touching the ground as well as the fully flamed belly covering that Riggle normally used for sponsor decals. (Photo Courtesy Ted Pappacena/dragracingimagery.com)*

Hurst always brought a large contingency of vehicles to the Indianapolis 500 race. This 1968 photo was included on the front of the catalog and showed all of the Hurst-branded vehicles in attendance. (Photo Courtesy Mark Fletcher Collection)

In front of the Hurst building, the 1968 car is loaded on the ramp truck and ready to drive to the next event. (Photo Courtesy Bill McDonnell Sr. Collection)

Puerto Rico 1968

Bob repainted the 1968 *Hemi Under Glass* a metallic gold paint scheme and used white trim when they made a trip to San Juan, Puerto Rico, for a racing and promotional event in 1968. The design featured a massive Hurst shifter painted on each side with the common round 4-speed ball. While it was very striking, George Hurst was not pleased with this departure from the previous black and gold color scheme. This trip was the only time the car was in this short-lived paint scheme.

Linda Vaughn and Bob were first scheduled to hand out photos and sign autographs at the local J. C. Penney store. The appearance of both Linda and the *Hemi Under Glass* was advertised in the local paper, and the event drew a large crowd.

One of the young men decided to pinch Linda. It certainly got her attention, and she swiftly removed her high-heeled shoe and hit the young man in the center of his forehead with the shoe's heel. Most of the crowd stared in amazement, and they all remained perfect gentlemen for the rest of the visit.

The race and the exhibition run took place the following day. Hurst employee Charlie Hopkins came along to help with the car and was placed as a guest of honor in the passenger seat of the official 1969 SC/Rambler pace car. The track

When Hurst took the Hemi Under Glass *to Puerto Rico for the races, they also attended a store grand opening where both Bob Riggle and Linda Vaughn were swarmed by the enthusiastic crowd.*

Linda stands with some of the school children who came to see the Hemi Under Glass *at a Puerto Rico store opening.*

Bob lines up at the starting line to perform a wheels-up show for the spectators. The crowds stood on the hillside due to a lack of spectator stands at the track. (Photo Courtesy Bob Riggle Collection)

The Puerto Rican crowd was enthusiastic about the Hemi Under Glass. *It consisted of mainly young males, and Bob and Linda were often overwhelmed by the attention.*

Bob and a Hurst crew member wear Hurst Hemi Under Glass *T-shirts that Bob made for the events. (Photo Courtesy Bob Riggle Collection)*

George Hurst, Lila Hurst, and Linda Vaughn visit the military hospital in Puerto Rico while on the island to perform a show.

George Hurst addresses the crowd at the Puerto Rico track with Linda Vaughn in the background. (Photo Courtesy Bob Riggle Collection)

The Hurst team included Bob Riggle, George Hurst, Linda Vaughn, and others at the track in Puerto Rico in 1968 before the race event.

Before the exhibition run, Bob Riggle, George Hurst, and Linda Vaughn pose with the Puerto Rico track owner and his team. (Photo Courtesy Bob Riggle Collection)

Bob Riggle explains to a Blue Angels pilot the multiple controls he uses to maneuver the Hemi Under Glass *down the track. Notice how tight the quarters are due to the fire bulkhead that moved the seat closer to the dash in the 1966 car. Later versions of the* Hemi Under Glass *had the dash assembly removed to allow for more legroom for the tall Bob Riggle.*

owner had a blue 1969 Camaro convertible that pulled Linda's Hurst Shifter platform.

Bob and Linda both stood on the Hurst Shifter platform as it made a pass along the track. The rear of the stock Camaro convertible practically dragged on the ground because it was not suited to tow anything. Linda was always attired in tastefully revealing outfits and removed her jacket to reveal a bikini-style top. Bob sat in the front passenger seat for the return trip in front of the crowd because he realized that he would obstruct the view of Linda.

Back at Hurst's Home

Hurst performed at many military bases stateside. Johnsville Naval Base was located just down the road from the Hurst Warminster, Pennsylvania, facility. Each year the base held an airshow that opened the airstrip to both military and private historic aircraft. Hurst was asked to join in the festivities with George Hurst, Bob Riggle, Linda Vaughn, Jack Murphy, Doc Watson, and several local Hurst employees mixed in with the crowd of 150,000 people.

Bob Riggle with the US Navy Blue Angels in 1966 with the Hemi Under Glass *parked next to plane number one.*

Hurst Ownership Changes

In 1968, Hurst-Campbell went public with a stock offering. The two known partners (Hurst and Campbell) as well as a handful of silent investors were rewarded for their long hours and tedious efforts. With the newfound wealth came financial independence.

However, it came at a cost. The majority of the Hurst-Campbell stock was privately traded to a larger conglomerate of the Sunbeam Corporation, whose stock was traded on the stock exchange. Over the next three years, the Hurst-Campbell principals were systematically divorced from the company

Inc., into the Hurst-Campbell family. Airheart has been a leading manufacturer in the production of Safety Disc Braking Systems and Anti-Skid Devices for many years and is an important addition to the automotive oriented firm.

The firm also maintains close liaison with Detroit automobile manufacturers through its Hurst Performance Research Center in Warren, Michigan.

In support of Hurst's O.E.M. projects with Pontiac, Oldsmobile, Buick and Chrysler Corporation, Hurst Research conducts a continuing development program, working closely with the major auto manufacturers and O.E.M. suppliers.

An equally strong international public relations and publicity program by Hurst pre-sells their products to both the O.E.M. and aftermarket fields.

This balanced program of quality products, properly promoted and continually improved through extensive research enables Hurst to serve you* better!

*Manufacturer, Builder, Owner, or Repairman

(Left) Hurst-Campbell's ultramodern facility in Warminster, Pa.

(Above) First facility—A two car garage in Abington, Pa. where Hurst performed the first Lincoln Continental conversion—(Below) One of the first products manufactured was a bumper guard for VW Vans.

(left) William G. Campbell (Right) and George H. Hurst examine one of the 4-speed shifters with a new contour T-Handle.

George Hurst and Bill Campbell started Hurst-Campbell in 1958 over a kitchen table. The partnership survived 10 years before the company was purchased by outside stockholders.

Sunbeam Corporation started to buy stock in Hurst Corporation and eventually took control in 1969. Known for manufacturing and selling kitchen appliances and handheld electric razors, it felt the Hurst Hemi Under Glass was a liability to the parent company.

Hurst Shifter production remained at the Warminster plant, which became the headquarters for Sunbeam's automotive division.

The Hurst product offering was very diverse in the early 1970s. The success of the shifter products allowed the investors to purchase other automotive companies that had great products but lacked the public awareness and marketing prowess that Hurst provided.

in this first of many ownership changes.

Bob Riggle was one of many contributors to the success of Hurst. As an employee, the change of ownership in 1968 did not bring a financial windfall to the rank-and-file employees of the company. Riggle was tasked with continuing to boost Hurst's public image by displaying the *Hurst Hemi Under Glass* at the scheduled exhibition events.

Within a year of Sunbeam's leadership, the corporate lawyers determined that a 2,500-hp wheel-stander was a greater financial liability than any financial reward it may bring to the profit and loss statement.

George Hurst was no longer the owner of Hurst but still maintained a short-lived leadership role in the company. He approached Bob Riggle with a plan to sell the *Hemi Under Glass* franchise to Bob over time.

Bob became an independent contractor who retained 60

J. C. Penney sold Hurst products that were generically packaged to match its automotive accessories line.

This is what the 1969 Hemi Under Glass *looked like when Bob Riggle entered into a contract to purchase the franchise and the car hauler. For the first year, Jack Duffy continued to schedule the* Hemi Under Glass *events, and the car retained the Hurst name. (Photo Bill McDonnell Sr. Collection)*

Hurst had a wide variety of shifter lines by the early 1980s. The new ownership tried to create a good, better, and best approach to the market to boost sales. In reality, new performance car sales were declining, and the public was transitioning to small, higher-fuel-mileage cars.

percent of all bookings with the balance going back to Hurst as payment for the *Hemi Under Glass*, the ramp truck used to transport the car, and all spare components associated with the endeavor. The Hurst name then became a major sponsor for the car rather than an owner, releasing Hurst of any liability should an unfortunate incident occur.

Bob and his wife, Nanci, took over the event booking and scheduling duties that Jack Duffy, Dave Landrith, and the Hurst marketing department had previously performed.

By the fall of 1969, Bob Riggle met with George Hurst to review the purchase agreement and the financial progress achieved over the last season. Bob was pleasantly surprised when George handed him a completed contract that transferred all remaining interest in the *Hemi Under*

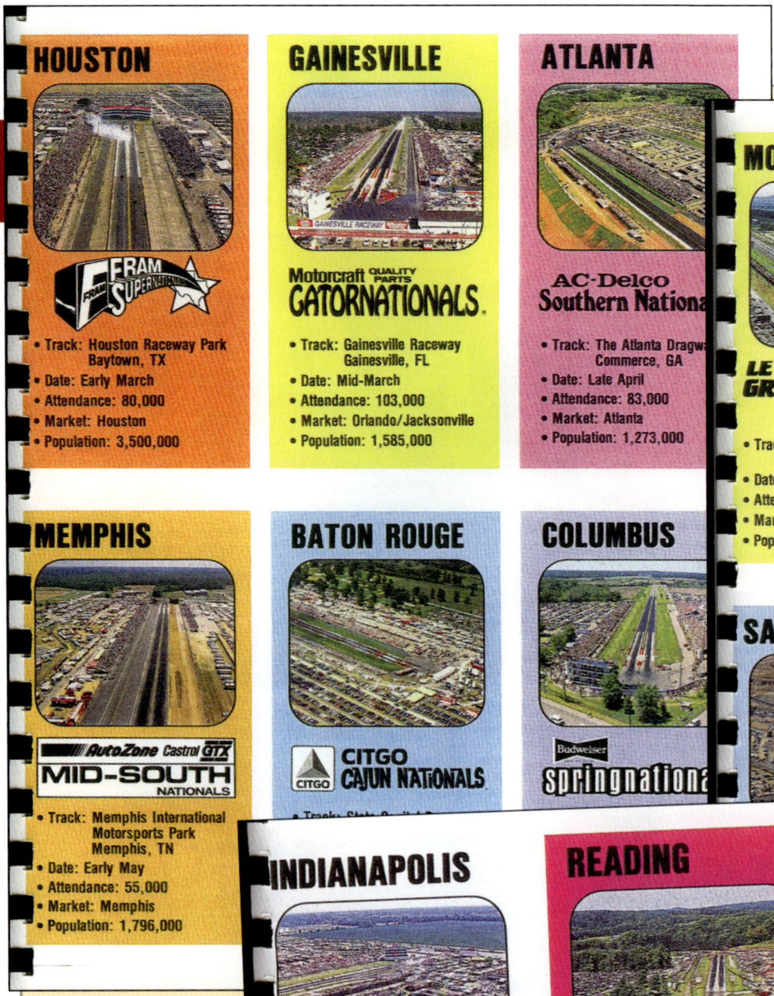

HOUSTON

FRAM SuperNationals

- Track: Houston Raceway Park Baytown, TX
- Date: Early March
- Attendance: 80,000
- Market: Houston
- Population: 3,500,000

GAINESVILLE

Motorcraft Quality Parts GATORNATIONALS

- Track: Gainesville Raceway Gainesville, FL
- Date: Mid-March
- Attendance: 103,000
- Market: Orlando/Jacksonville
- Population: 1,585,000

ATLANTA

AC-Delco Southern Nationa

- Track: The Atlanta Dragw Commerce, GA
- Date: Late April
- Attendance: 83,000
- Market: Atlanta
- Population: 1,273,000

MEMPHIS

AutoZone Castrol GTX MID-SOUTH NATIONALS

- Track: Memphis International Motorsports Park Memphis, TN
- Date: Early May
- Attendance: 55,000
- Market: Memphis
- Population: 1,796,000

BATON ROUGE

CITGO CAJUN NATIONALS

COLUMBUS

Budweiser Springnationa

MONTREAL

LE GRANDNATIONAL MOLSON

- Track: Sanair, St. Pie, P.Q., Canada
- Date: Late June
- Attendance: 54,000
- Market: Montreal
- Population: 1,181,000

ENGLISHTOWN

Budweiser Summernationals

- Track: Old Bridge Township Raceway Park, Englishtown, NJ
- Date: Early July
- Attendance: 103,000
- Market: New York/Philadelphia
- Population: 14,540,000

DENVER

Mopar Parts Mile-High Nationals

- Track: Bandimere Speedway Morrison, CO
- Date: Mid-July
- Attendance: 50,000
- Market: Denver
- Population: 1,095,000

SAN FRANCISCO

SEATTLE

BRAINERD

NorthStar Nationals

- Track: Brainerd International Raceway, Brainerd, MN
- Date: Mid-August
- Attendance: 82,000
- Market: Minneapolis/St. Paul
- Population: 962,000

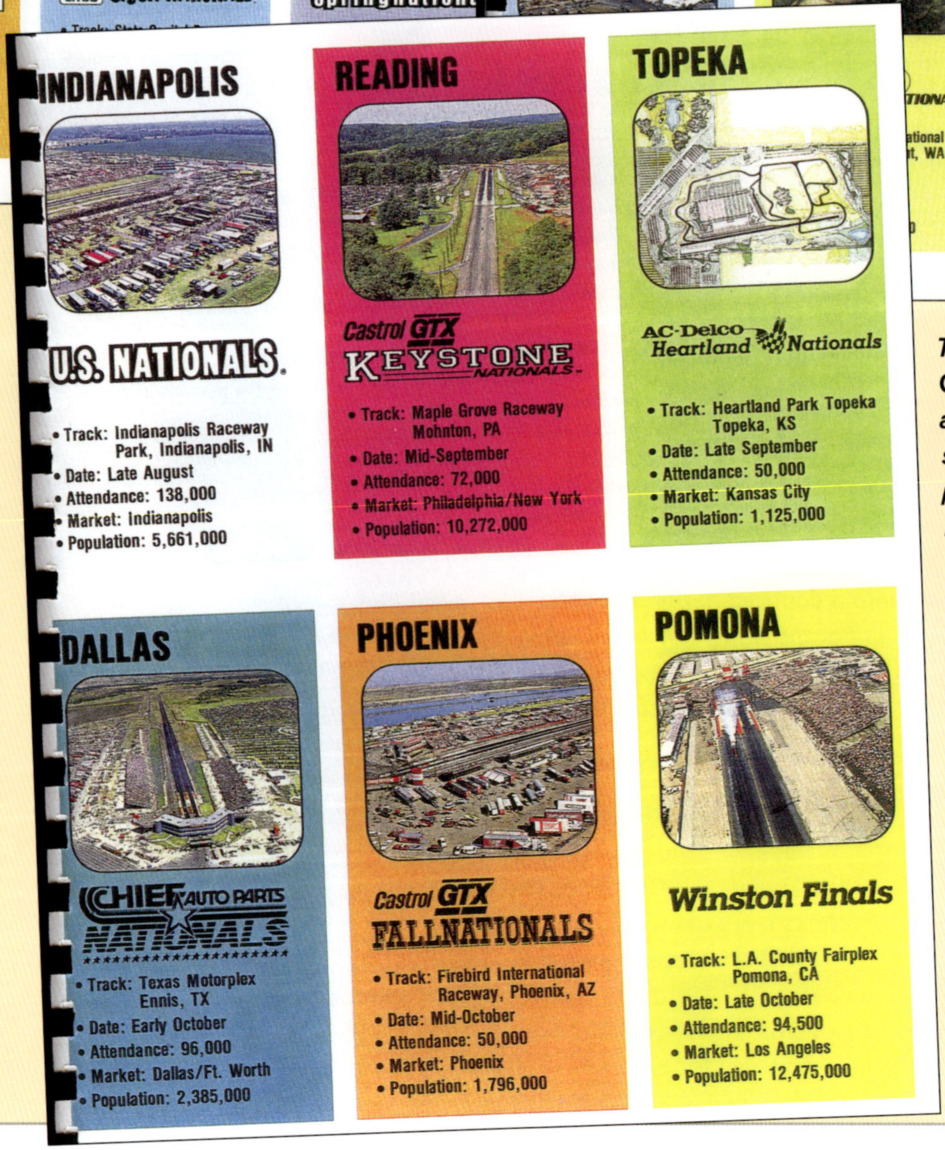

INDIANAPOLIS

U.S. NATIONALS

- Track: Indianapolis Raceway Park, Indianapolis, IN
- Date: Late August
- Attendance: 138,000
- Market: Indianapolis
- Population: 5,661,000

READING

Castrol GTX KEYSTONE NATIONALS

- Track: Maple Grove Raceway Mohnton, PA
- Date: Mid-September
- Attendance: 72,000
- Market: Philadelphia/New York
- Population: 10,272,000

TOPEKA

AC-Delco Heartland Nationals

- Track: Heartland Park Topeka Topeka, KS
- Date: Late September
- Attendance: 50,000
- Market: Kansas City
- Population: 1,125,000

DALLAS

CHIEF AUTO PARTS NATIONALS

- Track: Texas Motorplex Ennis, TX
- Date: Early October
- Attendance: 96,000
- Market: Dallas/Ft. Worth
- Population: 2,385,000

PHOENIX

Castrol GTX FALLNATIONALS

- Track: Firebird International Raceway, Phoenix, AZ
- Date: Mid-October
- Attendance: 50,000
- Market: Phoenix
- Population: 1,796,000

POMONA

Winston Finals

- Track: L.A. County Fairplex Pomona, CA
- Date: Late October
- Attendance: 94,500
- Market: Los Angeles
- Population: 12,475,000

Bob and Nanci created a booklet to show the venues they attended with the Hemi Under Glass. They hoped to add additional bookings to smaller tracks that were close by. Two or three events a weekend provided a good living for the family.

The Hemi Under Glass traditionally attended six major summer events to perform exhibition runs.

These are the six major fall events where they exhibited.

The* Hemi Under Glass *is just starting and is about three-quarters of the way up to the height that it will maintain for the length of the track.

Glass franchise to Bob as well as a check that returned the 40-percent portion that had been accumulated over the summer months.

Bob had always recognized George Hurst's generosity to others over the years but was now the recipient of this wonderful trait.

"George Hurst saw the value in people sometimes when they couldn't see it for themselves," Bob said.

After five long years as the pilot of the *Hemi Under Glass*, Bob Riggle was now the sole owner of this great icon of the racing industry.

During the next 50 years, Hurst Corporation endured a long string of ownership changes, product line splits, and brand mergers. All future owners of the brand directly benefited from the substantial efforts and growth that occurred in the first decade of the business by the enthusiast employees who established Hurst as a leader in the automotive aftermarket. No single individual contributed more to the brand's positive image than Bob Riggle.

As an independent racer and performer, the Riggles kept the *Hemi Under Glass* in the public eye for the majority of those same five decades. The corporation's concerns for a financial liability due to an accident were unfounded, as Bob was diligent in his safety management and never injured a spectator.

Bob proudly stands next to the 1968* Hemi Under Glass *in the gold and green paint at an early 1970s drag event. Note Gene Snow's* Rambunctious *1970 Challenger Funny Car in the background.

Bob Riggle and George Hurst stand with the naval base commander and the pilot during a visit with the troops.

Because of all the aircraft occupying the runway, the decision was made to run the cars down the long tarmac road that was near the fence and the temporary grandstands. As usual, Bob brought the Barracuda up with the nose pointed toward the sky and ran down the pavement. The run went well until the hard pavement turned to soft, wet grass.

As soon as Bob hit the grass, the car came down hard and dug the front wheels into the ground, which caused the car to gently roll over, but it was hard enough to break the massive rear window. By the time Bob was able to shut the car off, undo his safety harness, and fall out of his seat onto the ceiling of the car, several servicemen were there to help Bob roll the car back over onto its wheels.

After a quick check of the oil and a visual inspection of the car for safety, Bob drove it back onto the pavement and brought it up in the air again as he made his way back to the start. Once he stopped the car, it was surrounded by a crowd because everyone wanted to inspect the damage and shake Bob's hand.

Bob successfully campaigned the 1968 Barracuda *Hemi Under Glass* for three more years with only minor upgrades to its appearance. Each year, he changed the grille and taillight assemblies to better represent that year's production style. Hurst's Jack Duffy and Dave Landrith made

Hurst created an armed forces Jeep fully equipped with the Hurst Dazzler wheels and four Hurst girls: one to represent each branch of the armed forces.

This color photo shows the contrasting paint scheme of a gold car with green sides and gold-leaf shadowed letters. The paint job only lasted one season and was back to the more traditional gold, black, and white motif.

all the booking and travel arrangements for the last four years, Bob's wife, Nanci, helped manage the business end related to the car, and Bob traveled and drove the car at the events.

Bob enlisted a crew of different hometown racers to help him in these endeavors. One was his mechanic friend Fred "Waterbed" Miller. Fred was branded with the nickname when he attempted to repair his waterbed with a rubber tire patch only to wake up in the middle of the night in a sea of water. Luckily for Bob, he was much better at turning wrenches than he was at patching waterbeds.

Late 1960s, Early 1970s

By the late 1960s, more racers had built and were campaigning exhibition cars during the racing season. The crowds were being entertained by more jet-powered cars that were used to create a sense of excitement at the track.

Bob found that many of the spectators brought younger siblings or children to the races to have them see the *Hemi Under Glass*. No day at the drag strip was complete unless it included a walk through the pits and a chance to meet the daredevil drivers of the famous cars.

Bob made sure to emphasize the performance aspect of the *Hemi Under Glass*. Over the years, he perfected a process that helped get the spectators on their feet. Bob prepped the car and pushed it to the burnout box with the engine off. He ceremoniously waved to the crowd and climbed in.

Selling *Hemi Under Glass*

Although most of the Chrysler sponsorship was discontinued when Bob left Hurst, he was still allowed to get mechanical parts from the dealer network under the local racers program. He kept driving the same revised 1967 *Hemi Under Glass* Barracuda updated to 1969 trim that he retained through 1972.

"The car was getting tired and had a lot of flex from the constant torque to raise the front wheels and the hard landings every time it came back down to earth," Bob said. "I decided to sell the original *Hemi*

This color photo shows the original 1969 Hemi Under Glass *in a red-to-bronze color scheme. (Photo Courtesy Ted Pappacena/dragracingimagery.com)*

The last color combination of the updated 1969 Hemi Under Glass *is this gold-fading-to-red paint scheme. Bob Riggle and Chuck Poole remained friends and continued exhibiting into the 1970s.*

The* Hemi Under Glass *is warming up the tires before another nighttime run. Jim Wangers was instrumental at Hurst and introduced George Hurst to John DeLorean when he was the head of Pontiac.

Under Glass Barracuda to two brothers from Cleveland, Ohio, who proceeded to turn the car into a regular quarter-mile match race car.

"After that, I purchased a used Funny Car chassis with a Challenger body and redesigned the car to become a wheel-stander. The transition to the Funny Car design was rather easy, as the chassis I built still had the motor behind the driver. The chrome-moly roll cage placed my face and helmet at the center base of the windshield where other Funny Cars mounted the blower intake. I also included a window between my feet so that I could watch where I was going from the center of the car."

With the new car, he handed off some of the driving tasks to his friend and Mansfield neighbor Jack Ehrmantraut.

Hemi Under Fiberglass

For 1972, Bob purchased an AA/FC Funny Car with a fiberglass Firebird body from the Gay Brothers out of Texas. The chassis design was traditional in that the engine sat directly in front of the driver. Bob had Dale Emery drive this mostly forgotten car. Dale had spent the last year driving the *Flying Red Baron* wheel-stander owned by friend Gary Watson.

Funny Cars became more popular in the early 1970s, and Bob joined the trend. They were often called *floppers* because the lightweight fiberglass bodies danced and vibrated while the powerful engines pounded away at idle. It has also been suggested that the term is in direct relation to the bodies being hinged to the chassis in either the front or back to access the chassis. The car was designed as a match racer with the best time of 6.94 at 211 mph during the 1972 season at the Warner Robins track in Connecticut with Emery at the wheel. Although Bob owned this car, he never raced it.

Over the years, Bob had controlled costs by maintaining the car to the highest possible level because he knew that maintenance expenses were less than the repair costs when things broke. After one season, Bob realized that the arrangement was costing him more than 40 percent of the income. When the Firebird kept needing repairs after each event, he decided that it was costing more than he was able to make in the arrangement.

The Hemi motor and transmission were removed from the car and used by Bob in his new wheel-stander. He sold the rolling body and chassis to another racer and switched the engine to a new chassis with a 1971 Charger body that had the motor behind the driver to achieve the weight balance necessary for a continued wheel-stand.

Bob's First Retirement

In all of his years of racing, Bob escaped any serious injuries from any racing accidents. The *Hemi Under (Fiber) Glass* 1971 Charger had made an earlier successful run, and Bob wanted to race against Chuck Poole. As the Charger neared the end of the quarter-mile at more than 140 mph, Bob ran over a piece of metal that had previously fallen from another car. The rear tire popped and quickly deflated, which turned the car sideways and caused it to flip over. Bob pulled the chute and the car slid down the track on its roof. When he was almost to the end of the pavement, the car slid hard into a large light pole and broke the car's chassis in half.

The impact was so severe that Bob's Bell helmet was damaged as he hit his head on the roll bar, which knocked him out cold. Luckily, there was no fire, and the track team was quick to extract Bob and place him on a stretcher. As they loaded the stretcher into the back of the track's Ford station wagon, which doubled as an ambulance, Bob was conscious enough to reach up and grab the sides of the wagon to prevent the team from pushing him in. In his haze, he thought he was being loaded into a coffin and declared, "I'm not ready yet."

He promptly slipped back into unconsciousness.

Bob woke up in the hospital on

Bob replaced the Firebird Funny Car with a new 1971 Charger Funny Car body and chassis. The design was slightly thinner which added to the top speed. The fans liked the fact that the Hemi was once again a Chrysler Corporation product. Ironically, he is racing against Jack Ehrmantraut in his Challenger that eventually carried the **Hemi Under Glass** *name.*

The 1971 **Hemi Under Glass** *Charger leaves the line against Bill "Maverick" Golden in the Dodge A-100* **Little Red Wagon.**

The Challenger trim was painted on the fiberglass body to make it easy for Bob to update the look to the 1972 grille. One of Bob's two sons looks on while Bob goes through a final prep before a race.

a gurney in the hallway. No doctors were around, so Bob stood up and walked out of the hospital and went back to the track. When he returned, the team and Bob sorted through what was left of the parts. He blacked out again, and when he regained consciousness this time, he decided to go home and take it easy.

When Bob went to the doctor the next day, he was diagnosed with a severe concussion, bruised ribs, and internal bruising. He went back home and went to bed for two days with a throbbing headache. By the end of the week, he chose to take a break from driving for a while to recover.

By the early 1970s, Bob and Nanci had two young boys and a daughter, and Bob wanted to be there as they grew up. Bob chose to quit traveling across the nation with the *Hemi Under Glass* but was aware that both the public and the track owners wanted to see the car cover the quarter-mile on two wheels.

Bob's home track in Ohio was known as Dragway 42, which was located 10 miles north of Mansfield on Highway 42, which is also known as the Rainbow Highway. The track was owned by a fellow racer and friend Jack Ehrmantraut, who drove a fiberglass replica of an M-60 Sherman tank called *Hell on Wheels* for Bob Perry of Arizona.

Jack was also a part-time driver of Bob Perry's *Hells Fire*, a second tank-style wheel-stander in the mid-1970s, that was based on a

Patton-era Howitzer tank that shot blanks out of the cannon while the driver went down the track.

Bob built a new Funny Car–style wheel-stander with a 1972 Challenger body. He raced this version of the *Hemi Under Glass* against Jack who drove a 1972 Charger with the moniker of *American Graffiti*. For many years, Bob and Jack were booked together at events so that they could perform an exhibition wheel-standing match race between the two cars. In 1975, Bob moved from Ohio to Arizona, and in the process, he decided to sell the *Hemi Under Glass*–labeled 1972 Challenger Funny Car to Jack Ehrmantraut.

Jack and Bob came to a mutual agreement where Jack continued to keep the *Hemi Under Glass* name in front of the crowds with Bob as a part owner and occasional mechanic. This arrangement spanned 20 years and four different Funny Car body and chassis configurations.

Subsequently, Ehrmantraut also moved to Arizona and settled two hours south of Riggle in Tucson. By this time, Jack campaigned the *Hemi Under Glass* chassis with a 1978 Firebird body powered by an alcohol-burning blown Chevy. He continued to race with the *Hemi Under Glass* label on and off for many more years.

When the *Smokey and the Bandit* movie came out in 1977, Jack changed the name of the Firebird Trans Am to *Bandit*. His friend Tommy Maras ran a Plymouth Duster Funny Car painted like a police car named *Smokey*. They match raced with each other to entertain the crowds.

Then, Ehrmantraut once again relabeled the Firebird as the *Hemi Under Glass* and continued to actively campaign it through 1985, even

This Challenger was the Hemi Under (Fiber) Glass *owned by Bob Riggle in the early 1970s. Dale Emery was Bob Riggle's driver. The car had a Hemi engine in it while Bob owned it.*

The early 1970s Dodge Challenger body with Hemi motor was driven by Dale Emery. Funny Cars had become the bigger draw for the public, and Bob was successful when he combined the wheel-stander with a Funny Car to entertain the crowds.

Jack Ehrmantraut drove Riggle's Hemi Under Glass *for years. The two racers came to an agreement where Ehrmantraut used the name on a series of big-block Chevrolet-powered Funny Cars. (Courtesy Mark Fletcher Collection)*

Ehrmantraut campaigned multiple Firebird bodies with the* Hemi Under Glass *name. At this time the cars were campaigned as wheel-standers and performed as entertainment exhibits.

though the car continued to be powered by the big-block Chevy mill.

The Final *Hemi Under Glass*

The last Funny Car to wear the *Hemi Under Glass* label under Ehrmantraut was a confusing mixture of branding. The body was designed after the 1986 Dodge Daytona, which was a perfect choice to emulate due to the wind-cutting wedge body design that was exaggerated to fit the longer Funny Car chassis. Like the other Funny Car versions of the *Hemi Under Glass* wheel-stander, the driver saw midships with the cage visible at the front windshield area. The engine was aft of the driver to provide the weight balance needed to hold the balance for the car to easily stay up for the drag way distance.

This chassis campaigned from 1986 to 1993 was powered by the alcohol-driven blown Chevrolet big-block motor that covered the quarter mile in just over 9 seconds.

The name *Hemi Under Glass* remained on the body even while it ran the Chevrolet powerplant, and in this configuration it was invited to an all-Hemi match race. To keep the Hemi image, the owner altered the valve covers to make it appear as if the car had a Hemi powerplant in the chassis. When the other racers discovered that the engine was a big-block Chevrolet, Ehrmantraut was politely asked to withdraw from the competition. The Hemi part of the name was overlooked by the public, which did not diminish the entertainment value of the wheel-stander.

The* Hemi Under Glass *1977 Firebird was driven by Ehrmantraut and painted in the traditional gold and black trim.

The* Hemi Under Glass *Firebird prepares to race against the* Chevy Rebellion *Volkswagen pickup with a Chevrolet big-block motor. By the late 1970s, Ehrmantraut went away from the traditional gold color of the* Hemi Under Glass*. At this time, the Hemi part of the name was false advertising because a big-block Chevrolet engine produced the power.

Chapter 5

Other Wheel-Standers

By late 1965, the wheelstanding *Hemi Under Glass* was booked solid but was no longer a unique sight for the audiences. Not only did Shrewsberry go on to *L.A. Dart* fame but also other racers saw the value in being paid to bring their cars to the races. All during the 1965 season, many wheel-standers attempted to wow the crowds at local drag strips. Most of the cars were local racers who stayed close to home and didn't tour the national circuit.

Those who chose to attend the larger meets were often pitted against one another, and soon the exhibition wheel-standing cars were paired against each other in mock races. Generally, the script was agreed upon before the three-pass competition. The most enthusiastic performance had each car winning one pass and the final pass being the closest event. Although the speed of the cars was impressive, the ability of both cars to cross the beam at the quarter-mile mark still in the air was the ultimate show.

The first privately owned wheel-stander to be built was Bill "Maverick" Golden's* Little Red Wagon. *When the wheel-standers were first introduced, they generally ran solo exhibition runs. Over time, the drivers became friends and put on exhibition match races for the spectators. (Photo Courtesy Ted Pappacena/dragracingimagery.com)

1964 Dodge A-100 Built for Dodge as an A/FX Racer

Built by Jim Schaeffer, John Collier, and Dick Bransner, the brains behind the Dodge Truck Special Equipment Division were Collier and Schaeffer, who were both employed at Chrysler Corporation's Mound Road and Nine Mile Road Engineering Shack.

First driven by Jay Howell, then driven by Roger Lindamore who was also one of the Ramchargers drivers. It was specifically built with Dodge's blessings as a wheel-standing exhibition car based on the newly released Dodge A-100 cab-over pickup powered by a second-generation Chrysler 426 Hemi. At the end of the season, the truck was returned to Dodge, and Bill "Maverick" Golden was up for a new ride. Instead of a new vehicle, Bill asked for and received it from Dodge and continued to campaign it to the best time of 10.7 seconds in the quarter-mile.

For 1965, Maverick wanted to make some improvements to the truck. He took it to Sam Foose (Chip Foose's dad), where he welded the tailgate open and filled it with lead to add significant weight to the rear bias of the truck. The tailgate was reinforced further by a 1¼-inch straight rod in place of the side chains.

Steel pads were added on the back edge of the gate so that it sparked while going down the track. The tailgate acted as a wheelie bar for the truck and helped it maintain a three-point balance. The sparking metal of the tailgate as it dragged along the pavement was visually most effective at night and allowed the spectators to verify that the truck stayed aloft the complete distance of the track.

In 1966, Bill drilled 3-inch holes along the frame rails to lighten the A-100. Unfortunately, the truck became too unstable, and they needed to add bracing to keep it from twisting under the torque of the massive Hemi.

Second only to Bob Riggle and the *Hemi Under Glass*, the *Little Red Wagon* became a household name as the longest continuously campaigned wheel-stander with Bill

Another early entry to the wheel-standers was the Chrysler Hemi-powered Dodge Fever, *which was sponsored by Harris Sales in Boston, Massachusetts. (Photo Courtesy Ted Pappacena/ dragracingimagery .com)*

Golden behind the wheel from 1965 to 2003 when he retired. During those 38 years, the truck was severely wrecked on three occasions and was replaced by a 1965 Dodge A-100 in 1975. Both versions still exist today; the second truck has a racing pedigree of 28 years.

This poster was used to promote the appearance of the Little Red Wagon *at Rockford Dragway on Sunday, August 30, 1970. He likely participated in other exhibits at close by drag strips on Friday and Saturday night as well.*

This is a reproduction of an early Little Red Wagon *poster for October 10, 1965. At this time, Maverick claimed a 10-foot high wheel-stand. Within a few years, he promoted a 15-foot wheel-stand.*

"Wild Bill" Shrewsberry: *L.A. Dart*

Bill decided to leave Hurst and start his wheel-standing business in the fall of 1965. Sponsored by the Los Angeles Dodge Dealers, he built a car around the small Dodge Dart. Painted in distinctive red and white stripes, the 1966 Dart two-door sedan was Hemi powered. The motor was mounted behind the driver ahead of the rear axle in a similar layout to the *Hemi Under Glass*. It had no back window, and the headers exited underneath the rear axle.

During the first season, the 1966 car was involved in a rollover accident, and the car was replaced with the new-for-1967-bodystyle Dart in the strongest body design of a two-door post configuration. Shrewsberry campaigned this car for three years with minor updates to resemble the current-model-year changes.

Eventually, this car was replaced by a 1970-bodystyle hardtop with the massive Hemi engine placed behind the rear axle. It had Zoomie-style headers that pointed upward from the motor through the open trunk cavity of the car. Bill eventually graduated to a fiberglass-bodied 1972 Dodge Challenger that was built on a Funny Car frame with a Dodge Hemi motor that hung precariously behind the rear axle.

The Dodge and Plymouth friendly sibling rivalry was emphasized by the two drivers who once worked together and now often competed for the spotlight. By the late 1970s, Shrewsberry drove the 1930 Ford Model A delivery truck sponsored by Knott's Berry Farm. Custom car builder Ed Roth painted the *Knott's Berry Farm Wagon*, which was powered by a Chrysler Hemi and capable of more than 120 mph in the quarter-mile during its wheel-standing performance.

Bill Shrewsberry was the first driver of the **Hemi Under Glass*****. He then built and drove his own car under the*** **L.A. Dart** ***label. Both Shrewsberry and Bob Riggle grew up in Mansfield, Ohio, and knew each other in their teens. (Photo Courtesy Ted Pappacena/ dragracingimagery.com)***

Bill Shrewsberry (right) and Bob Riggle (left) were first coworkers and then became friendly rivals with the **L.A. Dart** ***and the*** **Hemi Under Glass*****. Both were powered by the venerable Chrysler Hemi and fed off the sibling rivalry of Plymouth and Dodge. Bob Riggle made sure to win the competition whenever possible. (Photo Courtesy Ted Pappacena/ dragracingimagery.com)***

Like many of the early wheel-standers, Chuck Poole drove a Dodge A-100 pickup with the motor moved aft in the bed. If one Hemi is good, then two must be better. Chuck had two in the back of his second three-window truck in this photo. He later sold the Dodge and switched the drivetrain to a similarly designed Volkswagen pickup.

Chuck Poole built the Volkswagen pickup wheel-stander when he went back to a single Hemi motor. He sold the Dodge A-100 to someone in Canada, where it was raced under the name Ecstasy. *(Photo Courtesy Ted Pappacena/dragracingimagery.com)*

By the early 1970s, the tracks looked to create excitement by combining racing venues in exhibition runs. Here, Chuck Poole drives the Hemi-powered* Chuck Wagon *against the infamous Ronnie Sox in the Sox and Martin Hemi-powered* Plymouth Duster. *(Photo Courtesy Ted Pappacena/dragracingimagery.com)

Chuck Poole: *Chuck Wagon* Dodge A-100 Pickup

Chuck Poole from Sacramento, California, was an early entry into the exhibition wheel-standing competition. His first vehicle was a 1965 A-100 five-window pickup called the *Chuck Wagon*.

After his *Chuck Wagon* Dodge A-100 was totaled during a wheels-up distance competition at Lions Dragway in 1965 that is detailed in Chapter 4, Chuck built a second wheel-stander with a 1965 A-100 three-window pickup. He upped the ante by installing two race Hemis in the bed of this truck.

It was rumored that this Dodge A-100, the *Chuck Wagon 2*, was also destroyed. However, it was sold to Sylvia Braddick in Canada, where she campaigned it under the moniker of *Ecstasy,* which was seen most often at Van Isle Dragways on Vancouver Island, British Columbia. It is believed that she was the only woman licensed for exhibition racing in North America at the time. The truck survives today and is awaiting restoration by its current owner.

Chuck switched to a VW pickup for his next truck because he did not like being confused with the *Little Red Wagon*. The chassis was the same Art Morrison design of his previous two trucks but was wrapped with the VW pickup body. He campaigned this version for many years.

George Shump: *Thunder Wagon* Dodge A-100

The *Thunder Wagon* was a Hemi-powered Dodge A-100 pickup truck sponsored by Chrysler Corporation.

This early photo shows the two most widely known wheel-standers competing head to head in front of a full crowd in 1967. The Little Red Wagon*'s tailgate was permanently welded in the open position and acted as the wheelie bar for the truck.*

Driver George Shump out of West Columbia, South Carolina, flipped out of control and demolished the truck at Cordova Dragway on June 11, 1966. Shump was unhurt and returned in 1968 after he converted the damaged truck into a unique A-100 pickup that had a literal roll bar over the top of the truck to facilitate a complete front-to-back rollover. The rear was bobbed with the slicks at the farthest-back point possible. The driver would pop a wheelie, causing the car to roll back like a turtle and then roll back onto its wheels. The car was captured on video at a large wheel-standers event in 1968.

The few times that it was seen in public, it appeared to have difficulty recovering from the upside-down experience. The concept of an injected Hemi was to eliminate issues with carburetion, and it appeared that the engine's oil system suffered oil starvation in the inverted position.

In one video, the engine even caught fire for a brief moment after it rolled over and back onto its wheels. The vehicle was short-lived and did not gain nationwide attention.

Bob Perry: *Fugitive* 1969 Corvette

Bob Perry, based out of Tucson, Arizona, recorded a 135-mph top speed in his popular 1969 Corvette *Fugitive* wheel-stander. Perry eventually sold the car to Gary Watson, who owned and drove the *Paddy Wagon* around 1973 and then campaigned it as the *Fugitive 2*.

Gary Watson hired Randy Curtis to drive the *Fugitive 2* for the next few years. Perry continued to campaign a wheel-stander that he introduced as an Army tank-themed vehicle called *Hell on Wheels*. The purpose of the tank was to connect with the young men who returned

Playing off the popular television series The Fugitive, *Bob Perry created this wild rear-engined Corvette with upward-facing chrome headers to entertain the crowds. (Photo Courtesy Ted Pappacena/dragracingimagery.com)*

After racing the* Fugitive *and the* Fugitive 2*, Bob Perry created the* Hell on Wheels *Army tank wheel-stander. He wanted to reach a new younger crowd who returned from their service in the military and attended the drag races in the mid-to-late 1970s. Jack Ehrmantraut occasionally drove the* Hell on Wheels *tank for Bob Perry. (Photo Courtesy Ted Pappacena/dragracingimagery.com)

from service. Occasionally, Bob Riggle helped Perry and drove *Hell on Wheels* at the exhibition events.

Gary Watson: *Paddy Wagon* Corvair Van

The well-known *Paddy Wagon* was built by Gary Watson and Bill Rodgers, of Corpus Christi, Texas, and driven by Gary Watson.

This radical Corvair van was powered by a 427-ci fuel-injected Chevy V-8 running on alcohol. Gary took the *Paddy Wagon* the distance of over 3,000 feet down the track with a top speed of 137 mph.

When the Corvair was no longer offered by Chevrolet, Gary replaced the Corvair body with a Chevrolet G-10 van body. He later purchased the *Fugitive 2* from Bob Perry and asked Randy Curtis to do the driving. Owning more than one wheel-stander allowed for double booking at an event that wanted to feature a wheel-stander match race for the spectators.

Richard Schroeder: Wentworth and Irwin AMX

The Wentworth and Irwin wheel-standing AMX was driven by Richard Schroeder out of Portland, Oregon.

It had a rear-mounted 390-ci fuel-injected AMC motor but was unfortunately destroyed in an accident at Seattle International Raceway (now Pacific Raceway in Kent, Washington) in 1972. It was built out of a regular production AMX and not built from one of the 52 SS AMXs as it was rumored.

The car was sponsored by Wentworth and Irwin Rambler and owned by Schroeder. Art Morrison, who became famous for his ability to create successful racing chassis, was the driver.

In 1972, Schroeder renamed the car *Dare to be Great*. Morrison was at the wheel when the car was destroyed at Seattle International Raceway in Puyallup, Washington.

Gary Watson of Corpus Christi, Texas, ran a Corvair van with a mid-engine 427 big-block Chevrolet. He later updated to the 1968 Chevrolet G-10 van with the same drivetrain configuration. (Photo Courtesy Ted Pappacena/dragracingimagery.com)

The Wentworth and Erwin *AMX was built with the engine in the back of the car specifically to be a wheel-stander. Based out of Portland, Oregon, and driven by Richard Schroeder, it performed primarily in the Pacific Northwest.*

Holly Swindle: *Backup Pickup* 1965 Ford Econoline

Holly Swindle of St. Louis, Missouri, began campaigning this 1965 Ford Econoline pickup in early 1966. It was powered by a fuel-injected Ford 428 engine and was reversed on the chassis with the cab in the back and the steering wheels under the bed. This wheel-stander was campaigned throughout the Midwest and was commonly seen at the

Wentworth and Irwin AMC promoted the wheel-stander AMX at the track and in its showroom. The car was used to draw in potential buyers for the AMC AMX, the Javelin, and the Rambler SC/Rambler.

Holly Swindle created and drove the unusual* Back-Up Pick-Up *that Bob Riggle rode down the track at the top of the front bed. He didn't anticipate that he would almost be bounced out when the front end came back down to the ground. (Photo Courtesy Galpin Ford)

wheel-standing-specific events. Bob Riggle was almost bounced out of the bed of this truck at one of these events.

Gary Kleckner: *Chevado* 1955 Nomad

This unique mid-engine '55 Chevy Nomad owned by Gary Kleckner of Monrovia, California, was one of the wheel-standing pioneers. Its mid-engine design had a drop-out subframe for easy access and servicing of the 427 big-block Chevrolet mill.

As the number of wheel-standers grew, so did the events where they raced against each other and entertained the race crowds. Soon, a day at the races wasn't complete unless it featured at least two wheel-standers racing side by side down the track.

Tommy Ivo: *Wagon Master* Buick

Even Tommy Ivo jumped into the exhibition business with his quad-engine, Buick-powered *Wagon Master*. It was a direct reaction to the *Hurst Hairy Hauler* Oldsmobile.

It was designed to billow smoke from the four-wheel-drive system, which was connected to massive slicks for the ultimate burnout. The car was a crowd-pleaser with its over-the-top design and unfathomable harmony of the four Buick mills. The *Wagon Master* was difficult to control and had its fair share of incidents with the guardrails. For this reason, the car's exhibition career was short-lived.

Two specific events changed the course of the wheel-standing exhibitions. By 1967, there were four active wheel-standers who decided to meet up in the expansive parking lot of the Los Angeles Coliseum. The group included Bill Shrewsberry and the *L.A. Dart*, Chuck Poole with the VW pickup *Chuck Wagon*, Bill "Maverick" Golden with the *Little Red Wagon*, and Bob Riggle with the *Hemi Under Glass*. It was arranged as a photoshoot for *Drag Racing* magazine.

Each car had a unique design and required different finesse to

***By 1967, the wheel-standers were often double-booked at events to run against each other. Bob Riggle stands next to the newly updated version of the* Hemi Under Glass.**

***Four friends assemble in Southern California for a magazine photoshoot. Clockwise from the top are Bill Shrewsberry with the* L.A. Dart*, Chuck Poole with the VW* Chuck Wagon*, Bob Riggle with the* Hemi Under Glass*, and Bill Golden with the* Little Red Wagon.**

bring it up to height. The photographers made many attempts to line up all four cars on their back two wheels for the photographer without much success. They were able to get one photo of the *Hemi Under Glass* and the *Chuck Wagon* both in the air with the *L.A. Dart* moving in the background but not yet airborne.

Although the drivers were competitors for placement at the races, they were primarily friends who shared design ideas and enjoyed each other's company.

The second major event took place at a Gary, Indiana, track with Bob Riggle and the video of wheel-standers. In 1968, Bob and a dozen other wheel-standers were invited to an exhibition race at US 30 Dragway outside of Gary, Indiana.

Billed as a wheel-stander match-off, 12 different cars were invited. Most prominently known were Bob Riggle with the *Hemi Under Glass*, Chuck Poole with the *Chuck Wagon 2*, "Wild Bill" Shrewsberry with the *L.A. Dart* in its 1968 trim, Bill "Maverick" Golden with the *Little Red Wagon*, Holly Swindle with the *Backup Pickup*, and Gary Watson with the *Paddy Wagon* Corvair van.

Video taken at the event that day shows a jovial group of daredevils preparing in the pits before performing for the crowds. After doing a few of the traditional wheel-standing match-offs, George Shump brought out the *Thunder Wagon* in its post-accident rollover pickup configuration.

After doing a few short wheel-stands, he lined up alone and brought the truck up on two wheels, goosed it, and flipped over onto its rounded roll bar. The truck then rolled back upright with flames emitting from each side of the motor. He turned around and returned to the starting line, where the safety crew made sure that the fire was out with an extinguisher.

Next up was the *Backup Pickup* with the chassis reversed under the Ford Econoline body. Swindle attempted to lift the front wheels but only succeeded for a short duration.

The Wild Thing *VW pickup had the rear engine cover welded flat, which was similar to the Dodge A-100 wheel-standers—other than it was much lower, restricted the height of the wheelie, and guaranteed a sea of sparks. (Photo Courtesy Ted Pappacena/dragracingimagery.com)*

Bob match races against a 1968 Chevelle that was built similar to the Barracuda with the engine behind the driver. It was common to run three match races during an evening of competitive drag racing. Bob made sure that his competitor won at least one of the contests.

Richard Hutchins ran this 427 Chevy-powered 1973 VW Pickup named **Chevy Rebellion**. *Here, he races at Old Bridge Township Raceway in New Jersey. (Photo Courtesy Ted Pappacena/dragracingimagery.com)*

As he returned to the pits for some adjustments, Gary Watson brought out the *Paddy Wagon*, and as he prepared to start his exhibition run, Bob Riggle ran out wearing his helmet and jumped in the passenger door. As Gary performed the wheel-stand, Bob stood up through the window opening and waved to the crowd.

At the far end, Gary turned around and Bob once more stood with most of his torso sticking above the dash of the van with all the spectators standing on their feet to see the daredevil performance. When the van came back down, the spectators saw Bob get a bit of a jolt from the impact.

Bob then jumped into the bed of the backup pickup with the tailgate facing forward and told driver Holly Swindle to go ahead. It took a few attempts for Swindle to perfect the wheel-stand because Bob's 200-pound weight that far forward changed the dynamics of the balance point for the truck. With each return to earth, Bob received a little jostle and tried to hang on to the top of the tailgate. On the return trip, Holly performed a single long wheel-stand that required some speed.

As he approached the grandstands and the starting line, Holly applied the brakes and came down hard. Bob said that all of his 200

One of the events Bob attended with the 1966 Hemi Under Glass *car in March 1994 was the NHRA Gatornationals in Gainesville, Florida, where Bob performed with many old friends in attendance: (left to right) Richard Cooke, NHRA Safety Safari; John Zenda, NHRA Historical Services; Bob Daniels, NHRA Division Director (has his back to camera); Steve Gibbs, NHRA; and Clark Rader Jr., owner of the National Trail Raceway in Hebron, Ohio.*

Bob Riggle, Clark Rader Jr., and Steve Gibbs are pictured at the National Trail Raceway in central Ohio. The event was at the NHRA Gatornationals in Gainesville, Florida, in March 1994.

Both Riggle and Bill Shrewsberry enjoyed fueling their rivalry in front of the crowds. Here, they meet up again with the Hemi Under Glass *Challenger (right) and the* L.A. Dart *(left) at the Indianapolis Raceway in 1973. (Photo Courtesy Ted Pappacena/ dragracingimagery.com)*

The Hemi Under Glass *in the 1968 trim was labeled the* Frantic Fish *between the taillights. Most competitors saw this view of the* Hemi Under Glass. *(Photo Courtesy Ted Pappacena/ dragracingimagery.com)*

pounds were both airborne and moving forward over the tailgate as Holly quickly slowed to a stop in front of the crowd. Bob admitted that he was a little shaken up by the experience as he jumped out of the bed, ran around the truck to be seen by those in the grandstands, and ceremonially kissed the ground.

Many exhibition drivers had a difficult time covering expenses—let alone making a living with the cars. The few cars that became well-known were able to capture the best bookings which paid the best. By performing at multiple locations over a weekend and then driving mid-week to the next location, only

Connie Swingle created and drove the Corvair Trash Truck *powered by a 427-ci big-block Chevrolet engine. Here, he is entertaining the crowd in 1969. (Photo Courtesy Ted Pappacena/dragracingimagery.com)*

a handful of drivers could afford to drive full time.

By the early 1970s, only a few full-time wheel-standing performers remained. The choices included the *Hemi Under Glass*, the *Little Red Wagon*, and to a lesser extent, the *Chuck Wagon* and the *L.A. Dart*. Most other wheel-standers had not succeeded in building nationally known names that stood the test of time in the memories of spectators. Many drivers continued to use their talents in a public racing career. Some were able to do it professionally, while others faded back into obscurity.

The more memorable the vehicle, the easier it was to get exhibition bookings. The kids loved the idea that their school bus could pop a wheelie. (Photo Courtesy Ted Pappacena/ dragracingimagery.com)

***Although the Dodge A-100 was one of the first wheel-standers to hit the tracks, the* Dodge Rebellion *name continued into the late 1970s, as seen here racing against the 1977 Firebird-bodied* Hemi Under Glass.**

Chapter 6

Revival of *Hurst Hemi Under Glass*

Bob and Nanci traveled with the 1966 recreation of the* Hemi Under Glass *to the United Kingdom to attend the Goodwood event.

Bob and Nanci Riggle moved to Prescott, Arizona, in the early 1980s and opened a motorcycle dealership. Bob became restless and desired to get back to the track. He purchased an AMC Gremlin with a 390-ci engine and 4-speed transmission that he raced in Arizona and Southern California. When he raced at the track, the announcer often introduced him as "The" Bob Riggle who used to race the *Hemi Under Glass*.

After playing with the Gremlin for a while, Bob built the first of what would be four replica *Hemi Under Glass* wheel-standers in his home shop. By 1993, Jack Ehrmantraut and Riggle came to an agreement that Bob would once again

The recreated 1966* Hemi Under Glass *was displayed at Bill Luke Dodge in Phoenix, Arizona, in the mid-1990s.

The 1967* Hemi Under Glass *was more of a restoration than a recreation. Based on the original car that Bob retrieved from Canada, it has the most original DNA of any of the four recreated cars.

campaign the *Hemi Under Glass* as a wheel-standing entertainment car.

Bob and Nanci also invested in some rental properties while he designed and built race cars for other racers as well. By the early 1980s, Bob was active in the local off-road quad and bike racing scenes and soon had a booming business through those with whom he raced. During this time, the itch to perform came back to Bob.

The 1968 recreated* Hurst Hemi Under Glass *was displayed extensively across America and even invited to the Goodwood event in Great Britain.

The recreated 1968 car has a primarily black bottom and a straight front axle. Often the year of the car is hard to tell from this angle. (Photo Courtesy Gil Rebilas Carshot/Thundering Images)

The 16 Cars named *Hemi Under Glass*

This is a list of the 16 different official cars that carried the *Hemi Under Glass* name:

1. 1965 Barracuda: the first version based on a production car
2. 1966 Barracuda: an altered appearance of the first car
3. 1967 Barracuda: the second chassis built from a body in white
4. 1967 Barracuda: the spare car (never used)
5. 1968 Barracuda: the No. 3 car with minor cosmetic upgrades (two paint schemes)
6. 1969 Barracuda: still the No. 3 car with minor cosmetic upgrades (two paint schemes)
7. 1972 Firebird: *Hemi Under Glass* (ex-Gay brothers car)
8. 1971 Dodge Charger Funny Car
9. 1972 Challenger: fiberglass body "flopper" (1971 taillights and 1972-appearing front)
10. 1972 Ehrmantraut Challenger: *Hemi Under Glass*
11. 1977 Firebird: *Hemi Under Glass* (raced until 1986)
12. 1986 Dodge Daytona: by an unknown chassis builder

Recreated cars:

13. 1966 Recreated Barracuda (first recreation by Riggle in 1992)
14. 1968 Recreated Barracuda (created in 1995)
15. 1967 Recreated Barracuda (from the original car around 2002)
16. 1969 Recreated Barracuda (Jay Leno car finished about 2011)

The Early 1990s Recreated Car Events

In the early 1990s, Bob Riggle was given a ride in the Chrysler Turbine Car while attending the Indianapolis 500. A Chrysler representative approached Bob and took him for the ride while he instructed Bob how to drive the car, which he then drove around the Indianapolis racetrack. The representative kept the registry of each person who drove the car. When Bob looked at the registry he saw that Hillary Clinton had also recently driven the car.

After selling the motorcycle shop, Bob went to work at a local car dealership as the service manager. Because of his mechanical skills, he sometimes helped the shop with unusual tasks. A Mazda RX-7 rotary engine's oil pan required a new bung to be welded into place. Before welding, he asked the shop mechanic to make sure that the oil pan was fully cleaned out.

During the last session of welding, the heat ignited the fumes in the inverted oil pan and the flame shot out the bunghole like a blow torch into Bob's face, which removed all traces of his mustache and eyebrows. The shop had a shower area, and Bob quickly took a shower and sprayed his face with the sunburn spray from the emergency medicine cabinet to take away the sting and care for his burn.

Bob Riggle was invited to ride in one of the few remaining Chrysler Turbine cars.

From there, he chose to take a vacation, but first, he hosted a cookout at his home for all of his coworkers at the car dealership. When Bob came out to cook the meat on the grill, he was dressed in a full fire suit with a helmet and a face shield. He told the crew that he should have been dressed the same way when he repaired the Mazda's oil pan.

Bob and Nanci hooked up a motor home with a motorcycle trailer and took off on a driving vacation. When he returned a few weeks later, the new manager wasn't very friendly, and Bob chose not to continue working with him. The owner of the dealership came over from California and asked Bob to stay, but Bob decided that it was time to do something else.

Building the First *Hemi Under Glass* Recreation

At the 1991 SEMA Show in Las Vegas, Bob met with Linda Vaughn who encouraged him to build another *Hemi Under Glass*. He soon purchased a 1966 Barracuda and began to recreate the car that he first drove for Hurst 25 years earlier. He set off to build an accurate recreation that used the same technology and components that were used in the original car. It took Bob 16 months to build the car in his home shop.

The first-generation 1964–1966 Plymouth Barracuda was based on the Dart/Valiant A-Body platform. This platform was a full unibody, which meant it did not have a separate frame or front subframe like other cars of the era.

The standard engine for the Barracuda when it was introduced was the 225-ci slant six. For buyers who wanted a little more power, there was an optional high-performance 273-ci V-8 that produced a respectable 235 hp. In comparison, the 426 Hemi used in the *Hemi Under Glass* started at 425 hp and was closer to 600 hp in racing form.

Even if the Hemi engine was placed in the front of the car, the subframe design would not survive the punishment of the torque on the body. For this reason, both the original and the recreated *Hemi Under Glass* cars were highly modified to keep the outward appearance of the original Barracuda. The donor 1966 car had the floor removed from the firewall to the trunk.

With Bob creating another Hemi Under Glass, *it was time for the marketing machine to fill calendar dates.*

The shell was placed around a newly created chrome-moly tube frame with a parts counter 426-ci Hemi and a heavy-duty modified 727 TorqueFlite 3-speed automatic transmission. In keeping with the original appearance and design of the first *Hemi Under Glass*, Bob installed a Hilborn fuel injection system, MSD ignition, and the same marine-application V-drive.

The rear-axle assembly was a heavy-duty GM unit from a motor home chassis that was customized to fit the narrower Barracuda body. At first, Bob used a 4-speed transmission but soon switched to a 727 TorqueFlite. He also switched to a 6-71 supercharger with Enderle fuel injection in place of the original Hilborn system. All of this was visible under the large rear window of the Barracuda.

Bob had a removable plexiglass version of the rear window created with quick releases for easy access to the drivetrain. This combination created an estimated 1,200 to 1,300 hp when it ran on alcohol.

The weight balance was essential to get the desired result. Bob calculated the weight of each component to keep the majority of the weight to the rear. The result was that 1,980 pounds of the total weight of the cars (2,960 pounds) rested on the rear wheels. Once the front wheels became airborne, the balance easily and predictably transferred to the rear slicks.

The interior was extremely sparse with the only two small gauges mounted low by the shifter to monitor the engine. The dashboard had no instrumentation, and it had a large rectangular hole in the center that aligned with a window in the firewall so that Bob could see the roadway while performing the wheelie for the length of the track. The driver's seat remained to the left like the production car. Although, Bob installed a passenger seat for the 1969 recreated car.

Each of the variations of the *Hurst Hemi Under Glass* had a stout wheelie bar with replaceable magnesium pads on the end. These created a colorful array of sparks that were most visible during evening runs. Like the original cars, Bob used Moon hubcaps in place of real headlights.

When the car was first finished, Bob had to get a few test runs under his belt. Living in a small community in northern Arizona has its advantages as well as its drawbacks. A friend in the local police force is always helpful to a racer. There was a long, straight road next to the local Ace Hardware warehouse that was virtually abandoned over the weekend. With the local police watching out for him, Bob made a few practice runs to fine-tune the performance.

Once the car was near completion, he dug out his old contacts list and made hundreds of phone calls to set up exhibitions for the new *Hemi Under Glass* that summer.

Getting the Show on the Road

Bob asked his youngest son, Jeff, who was just getting out of college, to help create the marketing materials that he and Nanci continued to use for the next 25 years. The material stated that it was provided by "the department of advertising and marketing," which was Bob and Nanci working from their kitchen table.

Bakersfield 1992: *Hemi Under Glass* Reborn

The first reintroduction of the car was held at the Bakersfield reunion in 1992. The NHRA organizer Steve Gibbs paid Bob to bring the car out for the crowd. Steve continued to help support Bob in the form of payments and a host hotel

continued on page 125

The Last *Hemi Under Glass* Rebuild

Bob Riggle and Bill Sefton decided that another *Hemi Under Glass* needed to be built. However, this time, it would be a nostalgic recreation that used a modern (for 2010) Hemi drivetrain.

During the build, the diminutive size of the 6.4-liter Hemi did not fully represent the reminiscent image through the looking glass that they had hoped for. Halfway through the build, they both decided to recreate the last version of the *Hemi Under Glass* with which Hurst was directly involved. The end result was the 1969 *Hemi Under Glass* complete with an original 426 Hemi under the glass.

The 1969 recreation started from a rough Barracuda that Bob was able to locate in Arizona. The rolling shell was virtually rust free although there were obvious signs of previous attempts at bodywork.

The 1969 version was stripped down in Riggle's Arizona shop. Here, the rolling shell hangs off the end of the four-post lift to install the front straight axle.

Once the front axle is installed, the steering mechanisms must be mounted. All of the Hemi Under Glass *cars had manual steering boxes as the front ends were light and easy to turn.*

The front-engine area looks incomplete without a motor. The roll-bar extends from the driver's compartment and through the engine cavity to the front of the car. This design meets modern safety requirements.

Riggle designed the 1969 car with a passenger's seat for the rare occasion that someone was invited to ride with Bob during one of his runs.

The rear-axle braking is accomplished with individual hydraulic circuits with two controllers mounted opposed to each other. Moving a single lever between the two master cylinders allows the driver to toggle braking to each wheel individually.

The larger shifting arm and the smaller braking arm are mounted in the center of the car, which makes it easy for the driver to reach.

The initial design for the 1969 car was to utilize a modern Chrysler 6.4L Hemi motor. On paper, the capabilities easily propelled the car down the track. In person, the smaller size of the Hemi powerplant was visually underwhelming in the back of the car.

Bob Riggle is reaching through the side window to work on the 6.4L Hemi motor. The smaller motor allows for easier access to the engine components.

The Hemi engine looks diminutive compared to the first-generation Hemi motors we are used to seeing in the back of the Hemi Under Glass *cars.*

Bob built the 1969 car in his workshop in 2010. Most of the drivetrain fabrication had been completed at that time.

Bob uses a four-post lift to raise the front of the car to the level he expects to maintain as the car goes down the track.

Bob designed the rear suspension to absorb the pressure when the car came to the wheel-standing position. This was to keep the rear wheels from lifting off the track when they came back in contact with the pavement while spinning at full speed, causing rear drivetrain breakage.

Bill Sefton owned all four of the Hemi Under Glass *recreations over the years. Here, he stands with three of the versions before the 1969 model was built. (Photo Courtesy Bill Sefton Collection)*

The Building Process of the Recreation Cars

When Bob Riggle recreated a *Hemi Under Glass* car, he did not imagine that he would end up building four of them.

He chose the 1966 car because he had the fondest memories in it as a new stunt driver for Hurst. The original car was a 1965 Barracuda that Bob re-skinned as a 1966 model because they shared the same Valiant-based bodystyle. For this build, Bob found a solid rust-free 1966 Barracuda that had lived an easy life in warm and dry Arizona. Bob kept a camera close by throughout his life and used it to fully document this first recreation build that took about a year to complete.

This is the recreated 1966 car with all four wheels lifted off the ground. If you look closely, you can see the pumpkin to the GM truck rear axle assembly that endured the punishment between the Hemi engines' torque and the spinning rear tires coming in contact with the pavement.

Bob Riggle started with a complete and fairly straight 1966 Barracuda for the first **Hemi Under Glass** *revival project.*

The bare shell was a solid car that did not need any rust repair or replacement panels before the build-up of the new chassis. The rear subframe was added, tied into the frame assembly, and blended into the front of the car.

Rear wheel wells have been radiused to fit the large rear racing slicks. The full roll cage is in place as well as the narrowed rear axle assembly scavenged from a used GM motor home.

A bare Hemi block is set into place to determine the mounting points. Weight transfer directly forward of the rear axle allows the car to wheel-stand without too heavy of a rear bias and still allow access to remove the oil pan to service the engine.

With the frame, roll bar, and suspensions fabricated in place, the car is moved for final body prep and painting.

The car is almost completed as the driver steering controls are added to the center of the car. The roll bar moved the driver forward a considerable amount and doubled as a protective firewall.

One major difference from the original 1966 Hemi Under Glass *car was the use of an automatic transmission in place of the 4-speed. Bob stated that the automatic transmission allowed for more driver control to keep the front wheels aloft for the length of the track.*

Although the engine was clearly visible through the large rear removable plexiglass window, the assembly process brought the engine from below the car with bolt-in motor braces.

The addition of modern disc brakes to the rear axle was imperative to slow the car down after the high-speed runs. Bob adapted the bolt-on brackets to hold the dual rear disc brake calipers.

The result was a disc brake conversion with dual four-piston calipers.

The four-piston Wilwood brake calipers allow for easy repair and servicing.

The custom rear cradle is completed and ready to be installed in the rear body cavity.

The Hemi engine utilizes a high-volume oil pump that plumbs into the custom sheet-metal oil pan.

The Hemi long-block is ready to mate up to the automatic transmission and intake assembly.

The Casale V-drive is the transfer case for this setup. It is designed to take the abuse of marine applications and is a solid component for each of the Hemi Under Glass *cars.*

The Building Process of the Recreation Cars *continued*

Back from paint, the mechanical components will now be installed before the final assembly.

Once painted, the doors, hood, grille, and trunk are all removed to provide access for installing the drivetrain, wiring, and driver controls.

The front area has added cross-bracing to strengthen the front sheet metal. The force when the front of the car comes back down could bend the front portion if not for additional bracing.

The painted body panels look like model car parts waiting to be installed. Bob replicated the statement of "A Rolling Research Laboratory" that was on the original car.

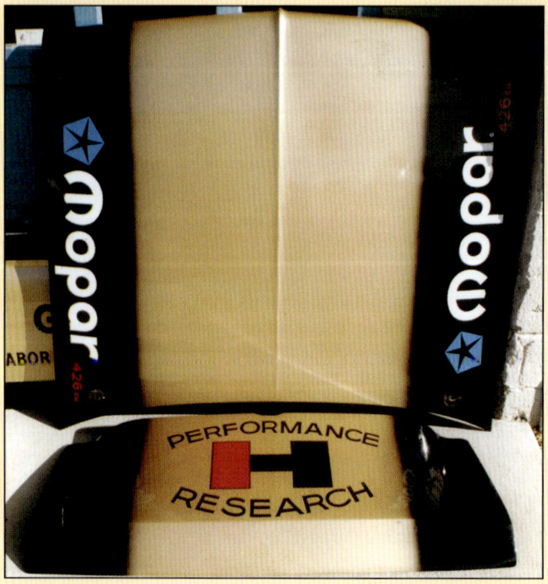

The hood and trunk are ready to install. Chrysler was a major sponsor prominently advertised on the hood with the Mopar logo.

Bob stands beside his finished Hemi Under Glass *car in the pits during the first season that he ran it in 1992.*

Bob Riggle and Linda Vaughn stand together with the recreated 1966 Hurst Hemi Under Glass *near the tower at the Winston Nationals.*

Riggle shows the finished cars to one of the sponsors: Doug's Headers in Southern California.

Bob's Recreation of the 1968 Version

When Bob built the original *Hemi Under Glass* cars in the late 1960s, he was confined to the current model offerings to represent the cars that Plymouth sold at the time. The original 1968 car that Riggle drove for the 1968 season was simply a 1967 car with a facelift.

When Bob decided to recreate a second car, he chose an actual 1968 car, which was in the second year of its three-year styling cycle (typical of that era). He found one that was another Southwestern car that survived the ravages of rust that normally plagued so many of the early Barracudas. Once again, Bob documented the complete build of the 1968 recreated car with photos.

The 1968 car started as a well-used but rust-free shell that survived by living in the dry southwestern states.

Solid floors and a straight damage-free body is the blank canvas that Bob Riggle chose to start with.

Once the floors and the wheel wells are removed, Bob will start to tube the rear and reinforce the subframes so that they can handle the 2,500-hp motor.

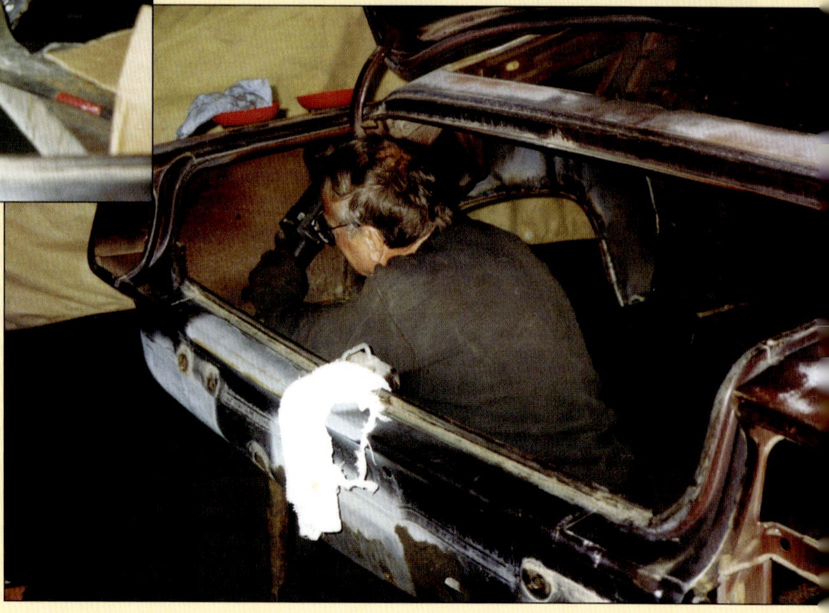

Bob has many friends and workers who participated in the build of the recreated cars.

The rear subframe is attached to the back of the rockers. A heavy-duty cross-brace is added across the car to strengthen the unibody.

Aligning the engine and transmission assembly with the V-drive differential is an essential element because there is no U-joint in the top connection.

The engine is mocked up with a scattershield for the initial design fit.

The car is supported on jack stands while the inner frame structure is welded into place. The rear subframe will be bolted as a single unit onto this frame structure.

The rear axle housing is a GM truck and bus unit that is adapted to run upside down and reversed in the rear-engine Barracuda.

The rear brake caliper mounting brackets are test fitted to the axle housing assembly.

Bob's Recreation of the 1968 Version *continued*

The top of the axle housing has been altered to a level surface. This is to allow for the installation of the transmission directly above the housing.

Cardboard is used to mock up and create a pattern for the custom tubs. The flat sheet metal will have ribs added to strengthen the curved steel.

Measurements are made to ensure the tub height is equal between the two sides before the final welding procedure.

With all drive components in place, the transmission scattershield sits directly on top of the altered rear-end housing.

The driver's seating position is moved forward to clear the drive belt assembly directly behind the fire bulkhead.

The firewall will be altered from the stock angle to adapt to the new front steering geometry.

Bob created a template for the inner rear side panels. These panels finish the inside of the body and frame the Hemi motor for the observer.

With the fabrication complete, the car is primed and prepared to go into the paint booth.

Returned from the painting process with the black over the top stripe adds to the traditional Hurst gold and black color scheme.

Bob Riggle has his hand in every part of the Hemi Under Glass *builds. The motor assembly is his forte, and he prefers to do the work himself using his first-hand knowledge of every torque spec for each bolt.*

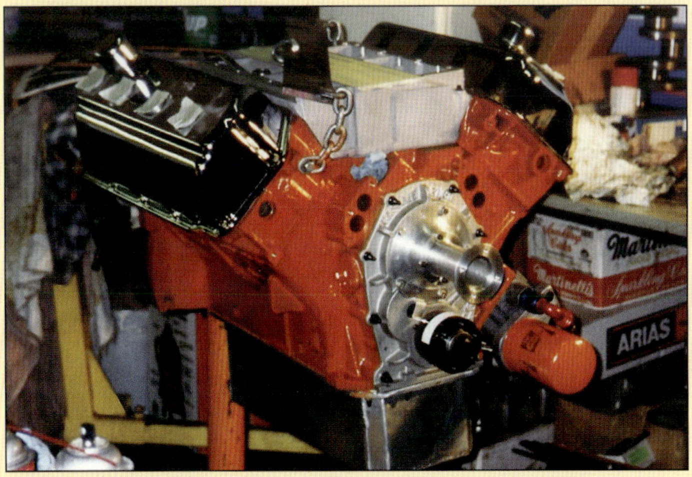

The motor is completed and waiting for the installation of the supercharger and fuel injection.

The motor is installed, and the painted car is ready for the supercharger and the drive belt to be installed.

Bob's Recreation of the 1968 Version *continued*

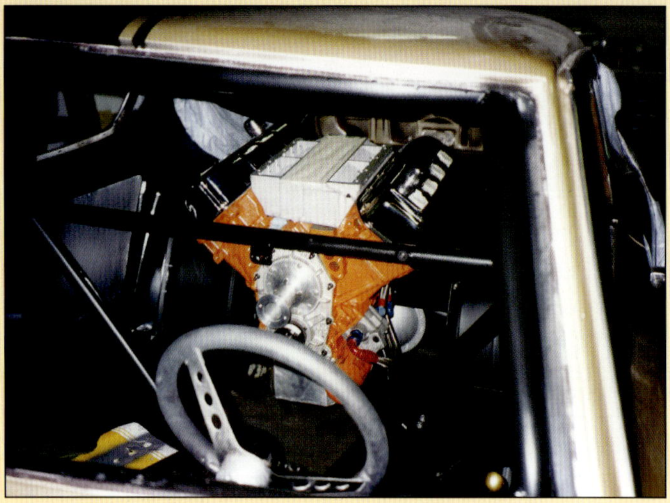

The large Hemi heads consume the majority of the space under the rear window.

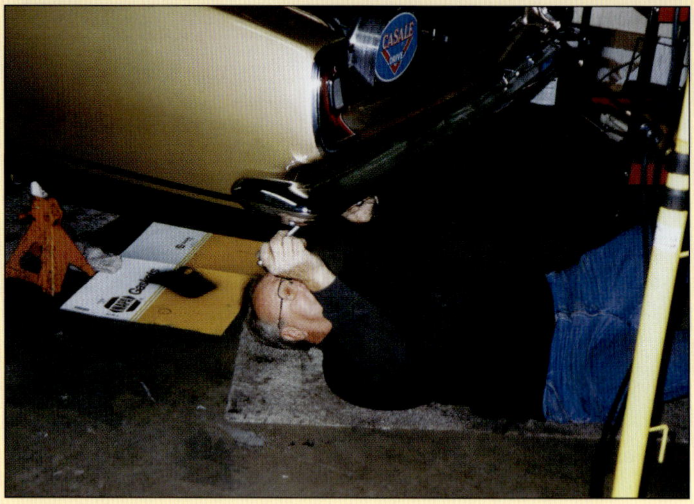

Bob installs the chrome rear bumper on the recreated 1969 car. The bumper will be protected from the pavement by the large wheelie bar assembly that will also be added.

The Hurst lettering was hand-painted on each panel of the car. Only the sponsors' emblems were applied as decals.

The 1968 Hemi Under Glass *nears completion. The engine bulkhead is one of the last components to fabricate and bolt in.*

The motor is completed with the addition of the fuel injection, front-drive pullies and belt, and the air scoop.

The engine drive belt comes within inches of the roll bar. The driver will have 2,500 hp spooling up 8 inches behind his seat.

The finished V-drive assembly is a polished and painted showpiece. It is hidden from the spectators' view unless the trunk lid is open.

The dashboard has been removed and the interior has a minimum of appointments.

Bob's Recreation of the 1968 Version *continued*

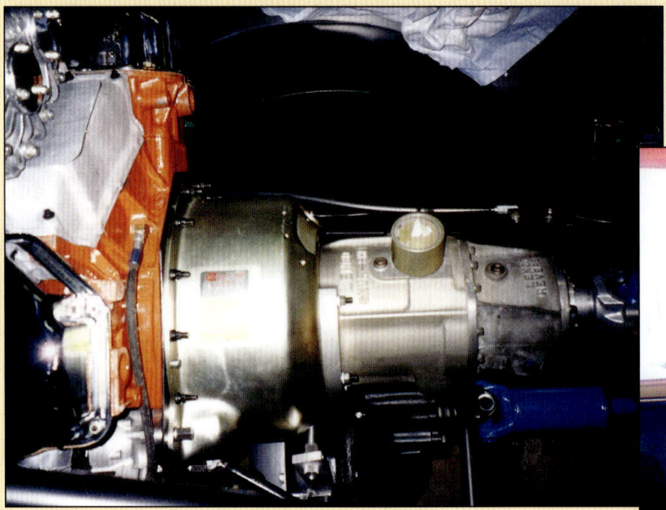

The transmission is cable-controlled, and this setup includes a U-joint on both the transmission output shaft as well as the rear pinion.

Bob inspects the body and paint while the glass and window trim are installed.

The finished car is driven out of the shop for the first time. Bob gives his signature "thumbs-up" as he drives away for a quick run.

The 1968 car sits outside the shop on the first day it was completed. Only the bulkhead firewall needs to be mounted to protect the driver.

room for events that the *Hemi Under Glass* attended until Steve retired in 2017.

Nanci often traveled with Bob from June through the fall, as she was involved with the school board during the school year. From Bakersfield, they went on to Indianapolis. At the event, it was determined that the roll cage needed to be updated to the current standard for the car's estimated elapsed time. Bob was allowed to make a short pass but had to keep the time slow to remain legal.

Bob approached the starting line. Each time he hit the gas, the car rose up and lurched forward, which brought the crowd to its feet. Bob remembered that he staged at the lights and brought the Hemi from its uneven idle to a melodic 5,000 rpm. As the light turned green, Bob dumped the clutch, began in second gear, and smoothly brought up the nose. As he continued down the track, he shifted each gear, and the crowd rose to watch the car remain airborne for the complete distance. For the youngsters in attendance, this was a new experience, but for those alive in the late 1960s (and the car's pilot), this was an adrenaline-filled memory relived.

Sitting in the pits at Indianapolis, Jeff watched as a gentleman introduced himself to Bob. The individual was from a neighboring racetrack. Bob committed to three additional bookings at the event. When the family finally arrived back home in Arizona after the late-May festivities, Jeff, who was in his early 20s at the time, told Nanci that he hadn't realized his dad was so famous and popular!

Once Bob returned to the shop, he rebuilt the roll cage to meet current requirements.

The recreated 1966 car was unveiled at the 1992 US Nationals at Indy. Bob was required to upgrade the roll bar before he made any official runs.

The Recreated 1968 *Hemi Under Glass*

Unlike the first set of *Hemi Under Glass* cars, Bob was not constrained to build the cars based on the sequential years. So, in 1995, Bob began his next project based on a nearly rust-free 1968 Barracuda that he found in the Arizona desert. He chopped and cut until he had a shell to build the new full frame under the body.

Bob designed and fabricated the frame to directly tie into the existing body subframe and forward to the front bumper. This accommodated and supported the narrowed leaf spring front axle, which was scavenged from a mid-1960s Dodge A-100 van. This was the same design incorporated into the original 1968 *Hurst Hemi Under Glass*. Bob had special 3-foot-long front leaf springs made to cushion the sometimes-harsh landings at the end of the runs.

This version of the 1968 *Hemi Under Glass* took advantage of the newly available Mopar crate motor Hemis that Bob used as a platform to build motors to his specifications with Arias 10.5:1 compression and a specific custom cam grind. He mounted a GMC 6-71 blower that was under-driven by 8 percent and fed its methanol formula through a pressurized Enderle fuel-injection system.

When the *Hemi Under Glass* was first run with carburetion, the car would fuel starve due to the 30-degree angle that the car achieves on the run. Bob once again had an Art Carr TorqueFlite automatic transmission behind the monster Hemi motor. Letting the transmission do the shifting meant one less thing for Bob to worry about on the track. Bob set the stall converter for 5,000

Bob raises his hands in victory after running a wheel-stander for the Chrysler dealer group assembled at Painter Motor Company in Utah. He performed on a straight strip between a multitude of new cars. Even the slightest mistake would have proved to be very costly that day.

rpm and included a built-in sprag to prevent clutch failure when the rear wheels come off the ground, potentially over-revving the drivetrain.

You would think that a 2,200-hp motor driving an overengineered wheel-stander would require a locker-style rear differential, but Bob preferred to keep the GM motor home housing open. A Positraction rear end made it harder to adjust the direction of the car with the hydraulic hand-control rear wheel brake. The rear received oversized Wildwood discs so that the car could easily stop from the typical 140 mph when it crossed the finish line.

A Casale V-drive safely brought the power from the transmission to the rear end. The V-drive setup originated back in the 1960s after a few rear ends were broken when the spinning rear wheels came back into contact with the ground and quickly identified the weakest link to the drivetrain. The Casale V-drives were built for heavy abuse in marine racing applications.

Memories in the '68 *Hemi Under Glass*

Painter Chrysler in Nephi, Utah, hosted the regional 1996 new car dealer introduction event and invited Bob to attend with his grandson. More than 25 dealers attended from all parts of the Southwest region. A helicopter flew in with an Elvis impersonator on board. When the helicopter landed in the dealer parking lot, the dust kicked up, blinding everyone outside the dealer building.

When the wind calmed down, Bob was asked to make a run between a row of brand-new Dodge and Chrysler cars. Bob voiced his concerns that if he got sideways between the cars on the dusty parking lot, they would make a very expensive guardrail. The woman promoter in charge of the dealer event accepted full responsibility if anything bad should happen.

Bob made a run of 300 feet each way and wowed the Chrysler dealer principals in attendance. Once he exited the car, the dealer principals explained how exciting it was to see him run between a half-million dollars' worth of cars.

The Four Trips to the Goodwood Festival of Speed

The Goodwood Festival of Speed in England has become one of the premier events on the classic car calendar. It celebrates motorsports in

When not making the run for the spectators, the Goodwood crew provided a shaded area to park the car and interact with the spectators.

all its many forms, with individual cars participating in a timed rally event that occurs in front of the crowds sitting in the bleachers.

The first time that Bob and Nanci were invited to the Goodwood Festival was for the 1993 event with the 1966 car, but they were unable to attend due to scheduling issues. Bob appeared at the event in 2001, 2003, 2007, and 2013. Over time, the *Hemi Under Glass* proved to be one of the event's most popular participants.

"The event features a huge television screen for the spectators," Bob said. "I started back by the photographers, and I tried to keep the car up high when I went under the bridge, but I wasn't able to accomplish it until the 2013 event, as it required me to steer while the car was in the air."

During one of the events, he performed a wheel-stand in front of the grandstands. The magnesium pads sent a shower of sparks behind him. He didn't realize until the end of his run that the sparks started the bales of hay that lined the course on fire. The safety crew was on the spot and immediately extinguished the smoking bales. Bob made sure to thank the young men who then asked to get some pictures with him.

Both Bob and Nanci returned to the Goodwood event two more times with the recreated *Hemi Under Glass* cars in 2007 with the 1968 car and in 2013 with the 1966 Hemi car.

Another special event that Riggle attended regularly is the Mopars at the Strip (MATS) event each March in Las Vegas. Bob has been a regular exhibitor there and has made many passes for the spectators. The event has been renamed Muscle Cars at

Bob quickly puts his front wheels up. The course has a few curves, and his goal was to remain up while he traversed the course by using the individual rear wheel brakes.

Sparks fly when Bob brings the car to the full wheel-standing angle.

Once he went under the bridge, he brought the car up for the second wheel-stand on the run.

The aftermath of the burnt haystack. The fire department parked next to the burn to watch in case of any hot spots.

the Strip but still retains its MATS label.

According to Bob, driving the *Hemi Under Glass* was the best job in the world. It provided well for Bob's family, but it did not create long-term financial security. To subsidize his income, Bob performed small to large fabrication jobs from his well-equipped home workshop. He built race cars for other racers and helped them create successful designs and individual components. If it could be created out of steel, Bob was the guy to do it. The welder was his artistic paintbrush that allowed him to make his ideas practical.

Bob made sure to take a photo of Tony and Matt, the two young men who put out the fire in the hay bales. This occurred at the 2013 Goodwood event.

Bob returned to Goodwood in 2007 with the 1968 **Hemi Under Glass*****. As he left the starting line, he started a small shower of sparks.***

Bob Riggle has attended the Mopars at the Strip event in Las Vegas, Nevada, many times with the **Hemi Under Glass**. This year (2007), he brought the 1968 recreated car for the crowd's enjoyment.

The **Hemi Under Glass** is shown at the 2005 Mopars at the Strip event with Bob Riggle at the wheel. At this event, Bob was in his late 60s. He continued to pilot the Hemi for the next 15 years.

Bob waves to the crowd after another successful exhibition run at the 2005 Mopars at the Strip.

The Hemi Under Glass *comes up to a full wheel-stand height just as the rear wheels cross the Christmas tree. For many runs, the front wheels did not touch the ground until the rear lights broke the beam at the quarter-mile mark.*

Bob is towed back to the display area where he will park the car, interact with the attendees, and sign autographs.

Bob makes sure to keep his car approachable for the public. He is also extremely sociable and sets aside time at each event to interact with the crowd.

Bob displayed three of his creations together at his shop in northern Arizona. The two* Hemi Under Glass *cars are the 1966 (far right) and the 1968 (far left). Also shown is a customer's A-100 that Bob built.

Hemi Xpress

Bob fondly remembered the introduction of the Dodge A-100 at the Detroit Auto Show in 1964. The pickup version of the A-100 was shown with a fiberglass camper on it. In the mid-1990s, Bob received a call and was asked if he wanted to purchase a used A-100 truck and camper located in Phoenix.

After Bob purchased and brought the truck home to Northern Arizona, he sold the rare factory-optional camper for what he paid for the truck. He then stripped the truck, cut out the floor, tubbed it, and converted it to the *Hemi Xpress* with a 500-ci aluminum motor in the back bed just forward of the rear axle. He took the Dodge A-100 pickup down to Phoenix for certification with a chrome-moly roll bar. It was later sold to Marty Moore, and its location today is unknown.

One of Bob's favorite pictures of the *Hemi Under Glass* was taken as he ran down the main street of Nephi, Utah, at night. Each year, the Painter Brothers Chrysler dealership had a show run down the town's main street that was five lanes wide. Bob ran down the center of town, and the highway patrol blocked traffic at each end. The titanium blocks were new and created a massive amount of sparks that were captured in the photo.

At the 2005 Summernationals held in Englishtown, New Jersey, Bob broke the car's rear end, and the car had to be towed on a flatbed. The rear broke while Bob pulled the wheelie as he shifted into second gear. The rear end completely locked, and the front end came slamming down on the pavement. Bob was able to depress the clutch and save the rest of the drivetrain. This is when Bob switched to the GMC motor home rear ends. He never had another rear-end failure.

While in Bowling Green, Kentucky, in 2014, Bob commissioned artist Steve Skyback to draw the car. The original picture hangs in Bob's home, and with the permission of the artist, Bob had smaller copies produced to share with friends.

In April 2012 during an event at Beech Bend Raceway in Kentucky, the track manager was not familiar with Bob and told him to only perform a half run to be safe. Bob obeyed and ran 600 feet both up and back. When he did a later run, the manager told him to not do a run coming back toward the starting line but allowed him to go about 800 feet on the way down. By the last run on Saturday, he must have heard about Bob's history and told Bob he could run the whole distance.

Bob crossed the finish line in the air at more than 120 mph and kept going another 300 feet on the long, 4,000-foot track. When Bob returned to the pits, the track manager said, "Well, I guess you know what you're doing out there." Bob agreed and mentioned that he "had a little practice over last 30 years or so."

The *Hemi Under Glass* has been billed as the best-known wheel-stander. Over the years, Bob Riggle has been referred to by many different titles, including racer, stunt driver, wheel-stander, thrill seeker, pilot, and entertainer. However, to many he is simply called a friend. Bob is often asked how many wheel-standing runs he has done over the years. He failed to keep an accurate count, but it was most certain in the thousands—if not in the tens of thousands.

This painting was commissioned by Bob and painted by Steve Skyback. It is one of his favorite paintings and is hanging in his home.

Bob added titanium to the wheelie bar on the car. When he ran the nighttime events, the fans loved to see the immense trail of sparks that followed the* Hemi Under Glass *the length of the track. (Photo Courtesy Gill Rebilas Carshot/ Thundering Images)

2014 *Mopar Collector's Guide* Magazine Hall of Fame

"Bob Riggle will forever be attached to his famous black-and-gold ride, the *Hurst Hemi Under Glass* wheel-stander Barracudas, starting in 1965," as was stated when Bob was inducted into the 2014 *Mopar Collector's Guide* Magazine Hall of Fame. "Riggle initially shared wheel time with Bill Shrewsberry in the first 1965 version *Hemi Under Glass*, then took over driving duties completely for the 1966 season and continued to make exhibition passes across the country until 1969.

"Hurst withdrew its corporate sponsorship after the 1969 season, but Riggle continued to make appearances in the popular car throughout the early 1970s until he was injured in a Funny Car crash in 1975.

"In 1991, Riggle opted to bring back the good old days, building another 1966 *Hemi Under Glass* Barracuda and racing it at countless events before he retired once more in 2005."

Recreated Car: The Frantic Fish

Other than being paid for his exhibition runs and having his expenses covered while at the event, Bob did not have any big-money sponsors. Occasionally, he had an oil company or racing product company that provided free products for a decal placement on the car. Sometimes those companies also supported Bob with a little money to cover fuel to and from the track. Even Hurst provided money to help offset the cost of the trailer required to tow the *Hurst Hemi Under Glass* around the country.

Finding the Original 1967 Car

Around 1995, Bob was at a racing venue when a gentleman approached him while he was signing autographs. During their discussion, the man said he believed he had the remnants of the original *Hemi Under Glass*. Bob asked for more information and some photos, and the two agreed to meet a few months later at another

The Only *Hemi Under Glass* with Actual DNA from the Original

The 1967 car was recovered in extremely rough condition and stored away for years. Once Bob sold the first two *Hemi Under Glass* recreation cars to collector Bill Sefton, it was time to restore the 1967 car.

Bob got to work on this car but did not document the progress in photos as he had done so often in the past. Below are the completed photos of the car that show Bob's unlimited capabilities in fabrication and restoration.

The 1967 **Hemi Under Glass** *build photos were not available for us, but we were able to photograph the car in a studio setting.*

The 1967 version can be identified by the larger red portion to the taillights and thinner taillight trim panel.

The sounds and smells of a 426 Hemi under full throttle directly behind the drivers seat was unlike anything experienced in a street car.

The 1967 **Hemi Under Glass** *was created with the impressive fuel-injection intake with six tall air intake stacks.*

The 1967 car uses an Art Carr TorqueFlite transmission directly connected to the Casale V-drive that directly connects to the rear-axle pinion.

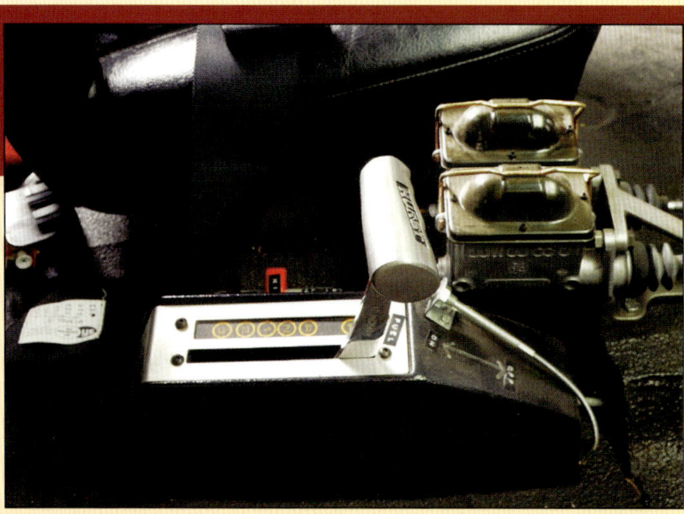

The Hurst shifter is a cable control to the automatic transmission. Bob wanted the interior to look period-correct to the spectators.

The 1967 interior is stark in appearance. The transmission shifter is to the right of the driver's hip with two-wheel brake controls that are used to help steer the car when the front wheels are off the ground.

The 1967 car has a spider web pinstripe on the front fenders. The Cragar five-spoke chrome mag wheels add to the nostalgic look of the car.

The side view shows how far forward the Hemi engine sits. The driver's area is rather tight, especially for Bob Riggle's tall build.

racing event. When Bob examined the photos, he recognized certain attributes of the 1967-bodied car that convinced him it was his old car.

At the end of the 1967 racing season, the car was returned to Hurst as a display and show car for Hurst and Plymouth. Once the proposed show schedule was accomplished, Sunbeam Corporation, the new owner of Hurst, considered it obsolete inventory, and it was sold to a racetrack owner in Canada.

Picking up the Car

At that time, Bob was busy traveling and campaigning the 1968 car. Soon, a deal was struck, and Bob was off to Montreal, Canada, with an empty trailer to retrieve what was left of the car. Even the recent photos did not prepare Bob for the project he was about to purchase.

The car's first owner after Hurst was the owner of the Naperville Dragway. He hired a young driver who wrecked the car more than once. Then, it was sold to another man who parked it, and it fell into disrepair. When Bob first recovered the car, it had a 440 big-block in it in place of the original Hemi. The good news was that it still had the hefty Casale V-drive unit in place. (Bob has photos of it when he bought it in Canada).

"I had no difficulty entering into Canada with an empty car hauler, but I had to be a little persuasive to get back into the United States with a hulk of a car that had no license plates, no title, and not even a factory serial number," Bob explained about the recovery of the 1967 car.

After a rather lengthy discussion, Bob was allowed to cross the border with the car that he last raced 30 years before. Once the 1967 car was home in Arizona, it was stored for multiple years while Bob worked on clients' cars between the scheduled events for the Hemi.

Back in 1967, the original car had a passenger seat, and Hurst conducted a lottery using the entrance tickets for the winner. A pretty young lady won the ride. She was a great sport and enthusiastic to take a ride.

"She enjoyed it so much that she yelled the whole time, and I could hardly hear the Hemi engine over her screams," Bob said. "Two of the recreation cars, the 1968 and 1969 versions, had a passenger's seat, and I have been able to take a lot of people for a ride over the years."

The ride of a lifetime has only been offered by Bob to special dignitaries, sports writers, or newspaper writers over the years. Sometimes these writers were completely unfamiliar with drag racing or the rich history of the *Hurst Hemi Under Glass*. A few of these writers surprised Bob by performing their due diligence, and they were very favorable in their assessment of the event, which was personalized by their first-hand knowledge of the car and driver.

Finding the Right Owner

In 2004, Bob had exhibited both the 1966 and 1968 cars for many years when he was introduced to Phoenix-area car collector Bill Sefton who specialized in rare Hemi production cars. They were at the annual Mopar Spring Fling event held annually at Woodley Park in Van Nuys, California, where Bob had the 1968 Hemi on display and attended the show along with Doug Thorley.

A man named Steve Kissle asked Bob if he had ever met Bill Sefton and proceeded to introduce him. Most of the attendees stayed at a local hotel in Burbank where Bill joined Bob in the lobby to talk about purchasing one of the cars. As both men were well-known to the Mopar collector community, they were frequently interrupted by the other showgoers. The meeting moved into the privacy of the hotel restaurant, where they continued to discuss which car Bill wanted to add to his collection.

After the meeting, Bob invited Bill to his home shop, where they came to an agreement that allowed Bill to purchase the 1966 car. Bill offered to purchase the *Hemi Under Glass* from Bob and have Bob continue to campaign the car publicly at events of his choosing. The two formed a loose partnership that allowed Bob to meet the car at the events rather than having to be builder, mechanic, crew, truck driver, and performance driver.

Bill Sefton soon owned both the 1966 and 1968 cars. Bob was ready to finally tackle the original 1967 car and was actively involved in the restoration when Bill showed interest in owning the original car once the restoration was finished. Arrangements were made for Bob to rebuild the car, use it for display, and race it in a few of the exhibition events that he had already committed to attend.

Completed!

Bob worked diligently to bring the car back to the version and look that the car had when it was originally campaigned. By early 2005, Bob achieved this task and made the yearly round of shows driving the newly-restored car. This car remains the most significant of the multiple versions of the *Hemi Under Glass*, having both been built and restored by the same master craftsman: Bob Riggle.

The 1969 *Hemi Under Glass* Recreation

When Bob left the employment of Hurst in 1969, he purchased the original 1968 car as the latest rendition of the wheel-stander. The 1969 version was built specifically at the request of Bill Sefton and was the last of the *Hemi Under Glass* recreation cars.

It was initially proposed to be an original-appearing car but with a modern, third-generation Hemi drivetrain. When Bob first met with coauthors Richard Truesdell and Mark Fletcher in 2010, this car was an active project in Bob's workshop. Sitting next to the car was a complete 6.1L 370-ci Hemi motor and racing transmission.

Somewhere along the line, it was decided that the newer Hemi motor did not create the wow factor that a supercharged and injected original-style Hemi sitting under the massive rear window inspired. The decision was correct as the crowds swarmed to the *Hemi Under Glass* and Bob due to the nostalgic memories formed in the 1960s. This car was completed in 2012 and was the featured car at the Hurst National events in Carlisle, Pennsylvania, as well as many of Bob Riggle's quarter-mile runs at national car club conventions.

Selling the '69 Hemi Under Glass

The authors were present at the 2018 Carlisle Hurst National event when Bill Sefton and Bob Riggle agreed to sell the 1969 *Hemi Under Glass* to Hurst fan and collector Joe Spagnoli from Chicago. Joe has a vast collection of significant Hurst vehicles that includes the newly discovered and restored Hurst Shifty Doctor 1969 Chevrolet repair van and one of two prototype 1974 Hurst Olds convertibles specially prepared as the Indianapolis 500 pace car used that May.

This 1969 car also stands as the last (to date) *Hemi Under Glass* car that Bob Riggle drove, with his final run on August 24, 2019, at the Gilmore Car Museum in Michigan.

The Next Owners

In 2013, Bill Sefton needed to trim down a large portion of his collection. He decided to liquidate the four *Hurst Hemi Under Glass* cars as a set and include all brand and marketing rights.

In January 2013, all four cars were offered for sale at the Chicago Mecum Auction. The group was bid to a no-sale at $750K. Dana Mecum addressed the crowd and said that the reserve was not met and the owner would take the cars to the Kissimmee Mecum auction, where they would be offered individually but the sale would not include the brand or the marketing rights to the *Hurst Hemi Under Glass* franchise.

Of the four cars, the 1967 car sold for the most at $300,000, and it was the only one with actual DNA from the first era of *Hemi Under Glass* cars. It can be argued that Bob Riggle's blood, sweat, and DNA is inherent in each of the recreated cars because he was instrumental in the design and build and he piloted each of the cars. The one constant from 1965 until today is that Bob Riggle had his hands in every car and appearance of the *Hemi Under Glass* for more than 55 years.

Which One Is Which?

With so many different versions of the *Hemi Under Glass* over the years, it is often difficult to tell the four years of Barracudas apart. This was the intent of Hurst; a similar appearance helped the public identify the franchise as a singular vehicle.

The 1966 car is easiest to distinguish with its ultra-large wraparound rear window. This car is the only version painted black with gold sides and a wide gold stripe over the top.

The 1967 to 1969 Barracudas share subtle differences with the Plymouth production versions. Unless you are a Barracuda expert, it can be frustrating to know how they differ from each other. Here is a quick tutorial on how to identify which is which.

The 1967 car is a gold car with a black stripe below the doors with gold at the bottom and a single black stripe over the top. Out front, it has the distinctive split grille finished mostly in black. The red taillights are C-shaped and surround the silver trim in the center. It has the words "Frantic Fish" in the rear license plate location. On the sides, it has a big, slanted red and black H logo that spells out Hurst. It also runs vintage Cragar chrome five-spoke mags.

The 1968 car is very similar to the 1967 car in appearance aside from how the large H logo is straight up and down and not slanted as on the 1967 version. The grille on the 1968 car is split with a silver center outlined in black. The taillights were changed for 1968 with the red lens being the smaller center part surrounded by a larger silver C-shaped area. It also runs more modern-looking Centerline-style wheels.

The 1969 *Hurst Hemi Under Glass* is painted gold with two black stripes over the top of the car, and the lower sides of the car are painted black without any gold below the black. The split grille in the 1969 car is all silver and no longer has the outlined areas like the 1967 and 1968 cars had. The

1969 taillight was the largest of the three years and filled the C-shaped area with the slightest intrusion of the total area with the center trim. The red and black H logo is straight up and down as on the 1968 car, and there is no lower valance under the front bumper.

Where Are the Cars Now?

The 1966 car was sold by Mecum and last seen in a private collection in Southern Florida.

The 1967 car is the only surviving original *Hemi Under Glass* and has been added to a private collection after it was sold at the Mecum Auction in 2014 for $300,000 plus fees to an unknown new owner. It has been sold once again in a private sale following a no-sale at the 2020 Mecum Kissimmee Auction for $225,000.

The 1968 recreated car was exhibited at more events since its creation in 1995 and has probably had the biggest audience of any of the different recreation cars built this century. It was sold directly to a private individual who occasionally displays it at car racing events.

The 1969 car has quickly become known as the "Jay Leno Car" due to its infamous run at Irwindale Raceway in California with the talk show host in a passenger seat. The car was damaged at this event and rebuilt by Bob Riggle before its ownership changed from Bill Sefton to Joe Spagnoli of Chicago, Illinois. Joe has kept the car in the public eye and displayed it at the 2019 Muscle Car and Corvette Nationals held at the Donald E. Stephens Convention Center.

After the Builds

Recreating and building the *Hemi Under Glass* cars is a major accomplishment that any hot rodder, fabricator, or car builder would be happy to accomplish in their retirement years. Riggle has recreated all four versions that he drove as well as a few other wheel-stander recreations mixed in with the four *Hemi Under Glass* cars.

Bob has also driven each of the recreated cars multiple times to bring the excitement of the historic wheel-standing era to the current generation of drag racing enthusiasts. Without his efforts, the *Hemi Under Glass* legend could only be experienced through the photos, film clips (some now available on YouTube), and stories that documented the events from more than 50 years ago.

Bob Riggle is deep in discussion at one of the many Mopar events he frequented in the 1990s.

The wheels and a few of the sponsor decals help identify this as the recreated 1968 car at Winston Dragway.

Chapter 7

The Jay Leno Ride

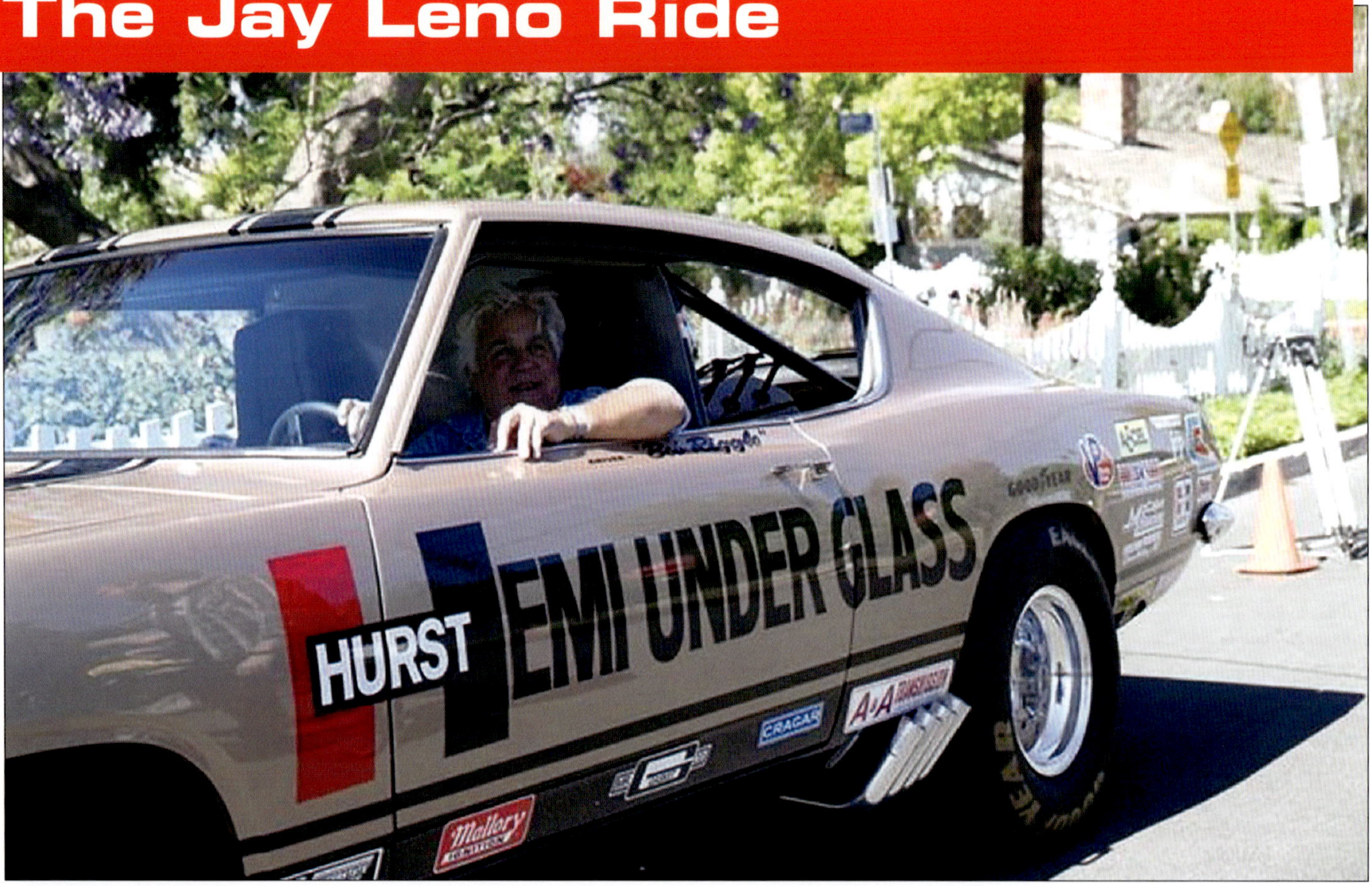

Jay sits in the* Hemi Under Glass *with his sleeves rolled up after filming. He was as excited to sit in the car as Bob Riggle was to be included in* The Tonight Show *skit.

Fourteen-year-old Jimmy Douglas was busy reading the April 1965 *Hot Rod* magazine with photos that showed all the details of the new *Hurst Hemi Under Glass* race car. Although the car was the inspiration of *Hot Rod* magazine's own Ray Brock, who conceived it as an A/FX (factory experimental) racer, the weight balance of the monstrous Hemi motor placed where the rear seat used to be caused the front end to defy gravity and stay up the full distance of the quarter-mile.

While 10th-grade Jimmy read the article in class, the magazine was snatched out of his hands by Mrs. Parker and unceremoniously shredded in front of the class. Maybe if Jimmy simply paid more attention to the lesson, he would do better on his tests. Mrs. Parker felt that it was time for Jimmy to quit being the class clown and apply himself to his studies. With a little more discipline and little less of his head being in the clouds, Jimmy may someday amount to something in life.

A few months later, in August 1966, most of his classmates planned to go to Shea Stadium to see the Beatles in concert. Jimmy (Jay) Douglas Leno prepared for a trip from his home in Andover, Maryland, to the New England Raceway just outside of Portsmouth, New Hampshire, to watch the drag races and see the stunt driver Bob Riggle at the wheel of the *Hemi Under Glass*.

It was almost 30 years before the now-famous Jay Leno finally met his idol, Bob Riggle, in person at a regional drag racing event in Las Vegas. Leno approached Bob Riggle in the pits next to one of the continuation cars that Bob had built and asked for an autograph.

"That'll be $1," Bob jokingly told Jay.

Jay handed him a dollar and Bob exchanged it for a signed photo of the 1966 *Hemi Under Glass* signed "Rapid Robert Riggle." Then, Bob promptly extended the dollar back to Jay and asked Jay for [Jay's] autograph at the previously established price.

Leno's Bucket List

When Jay was hosting *The Tonight Show* in the mid-1990s and found out that Bob was going to make an appearance at the Mopar Spring Fling Car Show in nearby Woodley Park, Jay asked Bob to bring the 1968 *Hemi Under Glass* car to the NBC studios in Burbank, California, the week before the car show.

Bob was unable to adjust his schedule, so they agreed to meet the Wednesday after the show. When Bob was shown the location for the quick wheel-stand, he immediately felt uncomfortable with the location and available distance. He asked the crew to open a chain-link gate at the end of the road and build a long wooden ramp to overcome the curb at the dead end. It was a good thing they did because Bob used the extra allotted space to bring the Barracuda to a stop.

In a skit prepared for *The Tonight Show*, Jay explained to the audience that he has lost a good amount of weight on his new beer and pizza diet. As proof of his weight loss, he walked up to the driver's side of the *Hemi Under Glass* that was conveniently parked on the street behind the NBC Studios. The camera showed Jay behind the wheel and he leaned forward as the car started to roll.

"It's not over, till it's over," Jay said.

Jay was then shown being pushed back in the seat as the *Hemi Under Glass* lurched forward to perform a short wheelie.

In actuality, Jay had traded places with Bob Riggle, who was dressed in Jay's traditional light blue work shirt and wore the helmet that Jay had worn. They showed the car doing about a 500-foot run and cut away as soon as it landed. In reality, Jay took the short ride in the passenger's seat and was left wanting to take a full ride down an appropriate track as compared to the short distance of this ride.

Bob was asked to stay for the show and hoped to be brought on stage during the show for an interview with Jay. This was not in the script, but Bob did get to sit in the audience for the taping of the show and saw the completed spot that was edited in time for the broadcast.

Ten years later, Bob called Jay Leno and told him they needed to finish what they started with the spoof video done while Leno hosted *The Tonight Show*. After many discussions, the date was set for mid-February 2016 at the Irwindale track. Because Bill Sefton had sold the other recreated versions of the *Hemi Under Glass* during the previous years, Bob brought the 1969 *Hemi Under Glass* Barracuda for the event, as it was equipped with a passenger's seat just for ride alongs.

The Infamous Ride Along

The *Jay Leno's Garage* team rented the Irwindale racetrack for two days to film an episode that featured the Banks Turbo Freightliner, which was designed and built to run the Pikes Peak Hill Climb in 2013. They asked Riggle and the *Hemi Under Glass* to join in on that prearranged event.

When Bob arrived and unloaded the car, he told the *Jay Leno's Garage* film crew that the track location may have been fine for the Banks truck to slide around, but it wasn't his preference for a straight-line wheelstand. They all discussed if they could move over to the adjoining drag strip or even the long parking lot. Bob had performed the wheelstand in similar constricted areas before, so after some discussion, it was decided to make a short run in the center infield.

When Bob and Jay first strapped into the car, the big Hemi was heard loping in the background.

Jay introduces Bob Riggle with the cameras rolling and explains how this has been a bucket-list item for him.

Once safely strapped in, Bob starts moving the* Hemi Under Glass *with Jay Leno as the passenger. Jay has his arm out the window and luckily moves it back inside the car.

What started as a 426 was built up to be a 468-ci Hemi with 2,500 hp. Atop the motor sat a GMC 6-71 blower with Enderle fuel injection. The race-prepared engine had a methodical speed-up and slow-down pattern to the idle. Sort of a *brumphhhh-brumphhhh* sound that is distinctive of a high-strung piece of machinery that is smoother at 5,000 rpm than it is at idle.

Jay strapped into the passenger's seat with his right arm casually out the window and his fingers grabbing the roof's drip rail. Bob's crew member, Max Merritt, attempted to snug down Jay's seat belt harness before the run, but Jay preferred to leave it a little loose.

With the first movement of the car, Bob hit the gas, and the front wheels barely came off the ground. Bob backed up, repositioned the car, and hit it at full throttle. The car

Even with the loud Hemi motor surging just inches behind their heads, Bob and Jay were talking about the upcoming run and how Bob planned to approach the starting point.

Bob goes down the field and launches the* Hemi Under Glass *in a cross-track trajectory. The plan was to pan across in front of the fixed camera position.

The Hemi Under Glass *starts its wheel-stand on a flat surface on the inside of the oval track. Bob was concerned about the short distance and was ready to shut down if necessary.*

The run is looking good as Bob and Jay pass the camera. By this time, Bob is measuring the distance until he needs to bring the front wheels back down.

popped right up for a short practice run. As the car went past the camera location and toward the far end of the paved Irwindale circle track infield, Bob felt the tires bouncing on the uneven surface. At this time, Jay moved his right hand inside the car and grabbed the roll bar next to the A-pillar. This proved to be a better choice than gripping the outside drip rail during the actual run.

What Could Go Wrong?

In the edited episode of *Jay Leno's Garage*, Jay jokingly stated, "2,500 horsepower on two wheels, what could go wrong?"

In the next few seconds, things quickly turned from hilarity to seriousness. They did a slow turn to face back toward the cameras, and then Bob gunned the throttle to invoke all 2,500 hp to attention. The front end came up smoothly to the 40-degree angle that engaged the wheelie skid plates. As they passed the camera location, Riggle let up on the gas, and the front end came down with a series of bounces.

Because the track was not level, the rear slicks flexed with the weight of the car. This oscillation interfered with the braking capability of the wheel-stander. Bob eyed the concrete K-rails directly in front of them and his decades of experience told him that he no longer had enough distance to safely stop the vehicle in a straight line.

Riggle spun the tail of the car around as he has done successfully many times before on flat track surfaces. Bob jerked the steering wheel to the left, but since the car was still oscillating and with the uneven track surface, the rear tires grabbed the pavement rather than sliding sideways as he anticipated.

With the outside tire sidewall flexing and rolling under, the car began to roll. Jay's passenger's side went down toward the pavement first. In the video, you can see that Jay's right arm actually goes out the window, and Jay brings it safely back inside just before that portion of the roof touches the ground. Because of the car's weight bias to the rear of the car, the car danced around, and the back end absorbed most of the blow. The video was shot from three the back end absorbed most of the blow. The video was shot from three different camera angles, and there is a point in the video where daylight is seen under the roof of the car while it is inverted and completely airborne.

The car continued to roll over the top, which impacted the driver's side, and then it luckily came to rest back onto the wheels. The car came to a stop with the front end facing away from the immobile K-rails that Bob was intent on avoiding.

The car only rolled over once, but the video shows it flipping three times through creative and dramatic editing. The car caught the driver-side rear upper taillight area first and danced around so that the passenger-side taillight area hit the ground next. The impact spun the car around so that when it stopped, it was facing the direction it came from and upright on all four wheels.

By cutting between the three outside camera angles, as well as the two different camera views mounted to the dash of the car, it appears that the car tumbled many times. You can also clearly see that because Bob's harness was pulled down tight, his movement in the cockpit was much more constricted than that of Jay, who preferred to have the seat belt straps slightly loose by comparison. With all the movement inside the car, both men were fortunate to have not suffered any serious injuries during the mishap.

The Irwindale track crew immediately arrived on the scene as Jay was removing his helmet. He came to the passenger's side and pointed across at Bob, who was detatching his safety harness. When Bob was asked his name, age, and location, he answered, "Bob Riggle, "I'm 80. Irwindale."

The rollover severely damaged the car, although both passengers were unhurt in the mishap.

When the safety man turned to Jay, he casually rested his arm on the door frame and said, "My name is Bob Riggle. I'm 80, and I am at Irwindale."

The track worker started laughing after he realized that they were both okay after the crash.

Before Jay could exit the car, the track crew had to bend the front edge of the passenger door in so that it could clear the trailing edge of the fender. Jay emerged a little disheveled, but he smiled and joked all the way. When asked if he was okay by his filming crew, Jay said, "Oh yeah,

The side that Jay Leno sat on received less damage than the driver's side. The rear weight bias concentrated the harshest damage toward the rear of the car.

The rear quarter and the roof section above Jay Leno's head show signs of scraping along the concrete track.

The rear wheelie bars are designed to support the weight of the car, but the sideways forces were enough to twist the steel like a pretzel.

After the accident, it was quickly determined that the car's body needed to be replaced because it was twisted out of shape.

I'm fine. It doesn't get more exciting than that."

The Aftermath

Jay turned his attention to Bob who had emerged from the driver's side of the car and asked if Bob was okay as well. They both hugged each other, and Jay added, "I do stuff like this every week."

They proceeded to walk around the car to assess the damage and quickly agreed that the car had taken a nasty hit during the rollover. Both sides of the body were heavily damaged. Bob stated that it was only the second major accident he had in 50 years of running all the various *Hemi Under Glass* cars. In their ensuing discussion, they both realized that their wives (Jay's wife, Mavis, and Bob's wife, Nanci) would not be happy to hear that they crashed a car at the track.

Jay's contract required that he visit the hospital after any unusual event that may cause him injury. Jay was taken by his manager, Sam Yamada, to the local hospital to be checked out. While he was there, it was reported that he did a quick comedy routine and had the emergency room crew "in stitches." Once he received a clean bill of health, Jay returned to the track about an hour later when Bob and Max Merritt were loading the crumpled *Hemi Under Glass* into the trailer. Once again, Bob asked Jay for

Jay examines the damage while his crew continues to film. He emerged from the car uninjured but a little shook up.

Bob and Jay compare notes and relive the rollover. Both agreed that they were not hurt and neither had informed their wives at the time.

his signature but this time on the passenger-side roof of the damaged car.

Bob and crew were sworn to secrecy about the incident, and the press was unaware of the near tragedy of the day. It wasn't until early June when rumors began in the automotive world that Jay had been involved in some type of major race car accident.

The first time the incident aired was four months later on June 16, 2016, on *The Tonight Show* with Jimmy Fallon. In this clip, the complete single roll is shown without being edited for dramatization. The whole incident spanned 15 seconds from the first movement of the car when its wheels launched into the air, and it concluded when Bob reached over and shut down the car's master power switch.

When the edited version officially aired on *Jay Leno's Garage* on June 26, 2016, it intentionally gave a more dramatic appearance that represented the car had rolled over at least three or as many as five times.

It seemed as if all of America had witnessed Bob Riggle make his biggest mistake on national television. With today's multimedia options, within a few short weeks, the edited version of the accident video went viral with almost 7 million views on *Jay Leno's Garage* YouTube channel, not to mention all the additional views on reposted car-related links. It is estimated that over 20 million Americans have witnessed the episode.

The Rebuild of the 1969 Car

After the show, Bob and crewmember Max Merritt loaded the damaged *Hemi Under Glass* in the trailer and towed it back to Bob's shop in Arizona. On the drive home, Bob was already thinking through the process required to straighten out the rear body section of the car. Once home, Bob spoke with Bill Sefton, the owner of the car, and they chose to find another used 1969 Barracuda body tub to rebuild the damaged car. They also chose to save the removed damaged body components to make a static wall display of the car for Bob Riggle's garage.

When the car was returned to Bob's shop, the damage assessment began. At first, the plan was to remove the driver-side quarter panel and the roof skin. Soon, it was decided to replace the inner roof structure as well.

As the stripped car was measured, it was determined that the unibody had been compromised from the front windshield to the rear tail panel.

Even the custom-built wheel tubs needed to be replaced. The rear housing and axles were unscathed, though.

The stripped-down car was cut at the A-pillar roofline. The roll cage was measured, was within tolerances, and was retained.

After the sheet metal was removed, the roll bar was wrapped in aluminum foil to protect it from the welding spatter when rebuilding the car.

This 1969 Barracuda body was used as the donor to repair the body of the 1969 recreated Hemi Under Glass. *The roof was cut at the front A-pillars and the body was cut in the rockers and transferred over to the frame of the damaged car.*

Bob found a rust-free Arizona used car body that was a good candidate and began the arduous task of removing the damaged portions and splicing in the new quarters, roof, and trunk lid. Due to the way the car pivoted on the rear sections, other than the passenger-side front fender, the front half of the car was primarily unscathed and was retained in the rebuild.

While Bob was reconstructing the *Hemi Under Glass*, he received a call from Jay's team who asked how quickly he could have the car back in California for another taping. Bob quickly finished the rebuild and went back to Burbank with a fresh *Hemi Under Glass* just a month after the disastrous accident.

The rebuild was a major undertaking that required Bob to fabricate from the subframe up.

Reunited for Another Photoshoot

For this event, Bob was taken to a rented mid-century home in the Burbank area where the crew

Once the rebuild was complete, the Hemi Under Glass *was once again transported to meet up with Jay Leno's crew in Southern California. Here, Jay points out where his arm was resting before the fateful run.*

Jay assured Bob that he was not angry about the accident and congratulates Bob on the rebuild. Car owner Bill Sefton looks on from the tent area.

Bob presents Jay with a Hemi Power jacket from the Walter P. Chrysler Museum for his good sportsmanship.

had set up shop. There was a young 10-year-old boy who resembled Jay Leno in his youth. A scene was filmed with this young man playing with a 1/64th scale *Hemi Under Glass* Hot Wheels toy in the living room of the house. The boy runs it down the track and then makes the car do a barrel roll at the end.

The crew filmed Bob making a few wheels-up passes in the neighborhood right in front of the featured home with the video cutting to the rollover sequence at the end. The city street was filled with parked cars on both sides, which caused Bob to be cautious with his wheelstanding activity.

After Bob made the first conservative run, the film crew wanted more. On the second run, Bob laid heavy into the throttle and the car popped right up, which scared the filming crew with the immense power and noise. By noon of the first day, the filming of the *Hemi Under Glass* street runs was complete.

The car was filmed with a jack under the front in the driveway to make it appear that it was doing a wheelie while standing still in front of the home. The scene then cut to the boy holding the *Hemi Under Glass* Hot Wheels car in the same position in the living room. The idea was that this all happened in the young boy's imagination with the Hot Wheels car, but like most youngsters, a vivid imagination was close to reality in the mind of Jay at 10 years old.

Bob explained that the scene was similar to the making of a movie with a full film crew, the neighborhood was filled with support vehicles, and the event was catered. Bob was able to interact with Jay while he was on the set, but the demands of the crew and the event did not allow the two to spend any significant time getting to know each other.

Bob enjoyed each of the three events for Jay Leno's show and feels that they were beneficial. You would think that he'd shy away from talking about an experience where he endangered the life of a well-loved celebrity. However, Bob is happy to retell the story of how it occurred and what he would do differently if he had been allowed to change the track environment. He does it all while smiling and laughing about the event.

Bob Riggle, right, saved the damaged passenger's side of the car and mounted it on a board for his shop. He stands next to Bill Sefton, left. When Bob met up with Jay Leno to unveil the rebuilt car, he brought the display and asked Jay to autograph it.

Epilogue

Bob and Nanci Riggle continue to attend racing events, and Bob may even get behind the wheel and wow the crowds. (Photo Courtesy Bob Riggle Collection)

Bob and Nanci now split their time between their winter and summer homes in Arizona and Ohio. They have continuously kept a residence in their hometown of Mansfield, Ohio, where they spend a good portion of the summer months. At this home, they are close to friends and family and the tracks that were the foundation of Bob's long racing career. During the colder Midwestern winter months, they reside in Northern Arizona, where Bob keeps a fully equipped workshop.

Bob has attempted to retire from piloting the *Hemi Under Glass* many times. Some of these breaks spanned multiple years and others were for only a few months. Whatever the future holds, Bob will never fully divorce himself from the *Hemi Under Glass* legacy. His larger-than-life personality has been indelibly inked into the hearts of the multiple generations who witnessed the crowd-pleasing antics of the *Hemi Under Glass* in their youth only to bring their children and their grandchildren to witness the one and only Hemi wheel-stander.

Throughout his career, Bob always has been able to put on a show. The impression of the car was only a portion of what the *Hemi Under Glass* had to offer. Bob was always in the pits with the car to interact with the active crowd. Young or old, Bob is eager to greet you with his James Garner–like smile and a firm handshake. All were welcome to touch both the car and the driver because he knew that this tactile connection created lifelong fans who would return to see the exhibition whenever he came to town.

As mentioned earlier, in the early 1990s, Bob began recreating the *Hemi Under Glass* cars in his

The Hemi Under Glass *was and has remained an iconic symbol of Hurst performance over the decades. The inaugural Hurst National event held in July 2017 in conjunction with the Carlisle Mopar Nationals featured the 1969 car. (Photo Courtesy Mark Fletcher Collection)*

A glimpse of the massive Hemi engine as seen through the open driver-side window. (Photo Courtesy Rich Truesdell Collection)

Bob attended the 2018 Hurst Nationals event at Carlisle in July 2018. He stands next to the 1969 (Jay Leno) Hemi Under Glass *that changed hands from Bill Sefton to new owner Joe Spagnoli at this event. (Photo Courtesy Rich Truesdell Collection)*

Northern Arizona shop that he built and drove back in the late 1960s. After building and campaigning three different versions of the icon, Bill Sefton purchased all three years of Barracudas (1966, 1967, and 1968) in a package deal. The agreement came with two stipulations. The first benefited Bill with a ride in the 1968 car, where he developed a true understanding of the car's nickname, the *Frantic Fish*.

The second requirement was most important to Bob: he would continue to drive the cars at a

Bob Riggle poses for a photo with coauthor Richard Truesdell at the 2018 Hurst national event. The first discussion for this book occurred at this event. (Photo Courtesy Rich Truesdell Collection)

Bob signs a diecast Hemi Under Glass *at the Hurst Carlisle Nationals in 2018. Bob is extremely appreciative of the fans and the life they allowed him to live by coming out to see his performances. (Photo Courtesy Rich Truesdell Collection)*

Bob Riggle's signature on the miniature model of the Hemi Under Glass *is set next to Linda Vaughn's signature on the real car. (Photo Courtesy Rich Truesdell Collection)*

Bob stands with the Hemi Under Glass during the transfer from Bill Sefton to Joe Spagnoli at Hurst Carlisle Nationals in 2018.

Bob Riggle and Bill Sefton stand with Joe Spagnoli (left), the new owner of the 1969 Hemi Under Glass at the 2018 Hurst Nationals, where the transfer of ownership took place. (Photo Courtesy Rich Truesdell Collection)

multitude of events that Bill attended annually. At a later date, Riggle built the 1969 car for Bill Sefton, which was initially envisioned with a modern-day Hemi, but they both agreed that the smaller Hemi motor did not give the needed visual presence to the car.

Midway into the construction, an old-school crate-motor Hemi was incorporated into the build.

Always the Daredevil

When not behind the wheel of a race car, Bob did a lot of desert racing on quads and motorbikes. While he raced motocross in a single-track race, he had difficulty passing a group of three other racers. As they came into a river wash, he passed them in the soft sand next to the hardened trail. However, Bob didn't see a large boulder hidden under a pile of sand.

When Bob's front wheel struck the large rock, he went head over heels and flew 30 feet through the air like Superman. When he landed, the bike followed the same flight path and landed right on top of him. It hit him in the back and knocked the wind out of him. He knew he was hurt and went to the doctor after the race. The doctor treated him for nine cracked and broken ribs. The ribs were treated, but a crack in his vertebrae wasn't diagnosed. Over time, a small protrusion formed on Bob's back from one of the broken ribs.

In March 2008, during one of his hiatuses from racing, Bob went to see a friend's son race the quad in Prescott Valley during the Xtreme International Ice Racing's Professional Tour. When his friend's son couldn't make the race, 73-year-old Riggle retrieved his riding leathers and promptly filled in, winning his class on the first time he had ever raced on ice. The local quad dealer offered Bob a quad to ride and all the required gear if he wanted to race competitively for the dealer the following year.

Transition of Ownership

In 2013, Bill Sefton liquidated some of the cars in his collection and reluctantly parted with all three versions of the *Hemi Under Glass* that Bob Riggle had meticulously assembled in his shop. Each car was transferred into private collectors' hands and is no longer campaigned.

Although the cars are occasionally shown at local, regional, and national car show events, the irony is they are only a partial aspect of what the *Hemi Under Glass* stands for. Without the heart and soul of the one individual who created and piloted each of the remaining cars, their importance is more of a historical design achievement that serves as a distant memory to all who witnessed the spectacle through the eyes of a child. Bob has been invited to attend these events along with the privately held *Hemi Under Glass* cars and anticipates doing so in the future.

Bob attended the Hurst National events held in Carlisle, Pennsylvania, in 2017 and 2018. During the 2018 event, with the rebuilt Jay Leno *Hemi Under Glass*, owner Bill Sefton, Bob, and potential buyer Joe Spagnoli came to an agreement for Spagnoli to be the new caretaker of the 1969 *Hemi Under Glass* Barracuda as well as the display of the damaged body panels from the Jay Leno rollover accident.

Last Pass?

Bob received an invitation in late August 2019 to the Oldsmobile show at the Gilmore Museum in Hickory Corners, Michigan. Spagnoli, the current owner of the 1969 *Hemi Under Glass*, invited Bob to do a demonstration run in the museum parking lot. This is the rebuilt car that Bob drove and flipped with Jay Leno on board in the winter of 2016 at Irwindale in Southern California.

Bob performed two short passes in the show parking lot to the amazement of the crowd. After a warm interaction with the attendees, Bob traveled with Joe back to Chicago before he boarded a flight back to Sky Harbor Airport in Phoenix, Arizona.

Major Accident

In a career that spanned five decades, Bob suffered few serious injuries. His luck ran out late into the night on August 29, 2019, when he was involved in a serious single-vehicle accident while traveling between Sky Harbor Airport in Phoenix and his home in Prescott, Arizona. He hit the edge of a roundabout near his home, which broke the left front wheel and caused the vehicle to roll over multiple times and all the glass to break.

All six airbags in his SUV deployed, and the vehicle came to rest on its side with Bob hanging from the driver's seat belt. He was trapped in the car for about 15 minutes, and the local fire department had to extricate him. Once the fire department arrived on the scene, they cut Bob's seat belt, which caused him to fall headfirst into the passenger's side of the car. The fall further injured Bob's back and possibly caused a concussion. The severity of the accident totaled the car and almost did the same to Bob.

Bob was rushed to the hospital in serious condition. He was

Bob stands between the beginning and the end of his long career with Hurst. He started with Hurst and worked on the **Hairy Oldsmobile** ***(left), and he performed his last exhibition run to date in the 1969*** **Hemi Under Glass** ***(right). The picture was taken in August 2019 just prior to Bob driving an exhibition run in the car. (Photo Courtesy Joe Spagnoli)***

treated and transferred to Phoenix for additional tests. After a prolonged hospital stay, he was moved to a rehabilitation center in Arizona for two weeks. At 84 years old, Bob suffered multiple broken bones, damage to his back and vertebrae, a serious concussion, and additional internal injuries. As always, he was determined to get back at it and went home against the doctors' wishes, where he began the journey back to his normal life.

The Recovery

As we collaborated with Bob on this book project, we chose to take a short hiatus while he slowly recovered before we re-engaged in the documentation process. After six months, Bob was once again animated in his sharing of stories, and he began speaking about participating in the race environment that has become his second home and family.

If you are fortunate enough to be in attendance and you see Bob Riggle walking among the crowd, feel free to approach him and let him know the significance that the *Hemi Under Glass* legend has made in your life.

The continued support from the fans kept Bob going during his rehabilitation process that dragged into 2020 as we completed the book that chronicled his more than five decades behind the wheel. The support from fans from across the world energized Bob to keep going and return from several retirements to do his next show with even more energy.

Memories Last Longer

He often saw the same people year after year. Never one to back down from a challenge, Bob started fixing things at a young age and believes he will still have unfinished projects when he closes his toolbox a final time. He has been industrious throughout his life and does not believe in idle hands. The biggest thing that Bob has built over the years has been the smiles and memories of everyone he has entertained. Those memories are indestructible.

Bob has been in control of a throttle for more than seven decades of his life, and he expects to continue driving as long as he breathes. He has traveled the world to entertain and interact with the fans he loves. Each day at home, he is either fixing or building something in his shop.

A typical day starts in the morning when he is often found enjoying coffee with friends and then helping a local customer who needs a repair to a bike, quad, or car. In between, he almost always has a restoration project to work on for a friend. Most

Bob was awarded this unique retirement chair when he was inducted into the Mopar Hall of Fame. The chair was created by Roger Painter and presented by Phil Painter at the 2003 Mopar at the Strip (MATS) event at Las Vegas Motor Speedway. (Photo Courtesy Joe Spagnoli)

Memories of Bob Riggle

Joe Spagnoli, owner of the 1969 *Hemi Under Glass,* and author and photographer Lou Hart shared the following memories about Bob Riggle.

Joe Spagnoli

How does one recognize a lifelong idol? Bob Riggle has been instrumental in my life and my love for the Hurst brand. One of my fondest memories of my youth was watching Bob pilot the *Hemi Under Glass* at US 30 Drag Strip when I was 10 years old.

I never imagined that not only would he become a mentor in my life but I would eventually become the proud owner of one of the *Hurst Hemi Under Glass* cars. More than that, I call him a dear friend.

In 2013, all four cars went up for auction to be sold as a single lot. I was saddened thinking that I probably couldn't afford one, let alone purchase all four of them. When they went across the block and didn't sell as a single lot, a light went off in my head that they might be sold individually.

Fast-forward to 2016. I watched the 1969 *Hemi Under Glass* roll over during the filming of an episode of *Jay Leno's Garage*. I thought that my chance to own the very last one had been destroyed in seconds.

Then, Bob decided to not only rebuild the car but also cut the damaged passenger's side off the rolled car and turn it into a wall hanging. What a great tribute to an iconic moment in time. In 2018, Bob had decided to sell the car and the wall hanging.

We all were at the Mopar Nationals in Carlisle, Pennsylvania, and met for dinner. That's when Bob and Bill Sefton, who had an ownership stake in the 1969 car, both looked at me and said that they couldn't think of anyone else better to own this car than me.

Immediately, a lump in my throat grew so big I couldn't talk! After consuming an entire adult beverage to dissolve the lump in my throat, I said that this was a purchase that I was going to have to sleep on. They both said they understood but if I decided not to buy the car, it was going to go up for auction in January 2019. They were both afraid of whose hands it might end up in. I had one comment, "Understood!"

The next morning at breakfast Bob asked me, "How did you sleep?"

I looked at Bob with the widest eyes and a boyish grin and said, "Like a baby—knowing I'm going to be the proud owner of the most iconic wheel-stander to ever run on a drag strip!"

At that moment, I witnessed something I never imagined would happen. Bob took off his glasses and wiped a couple of tears from his eyes and said, "I can't tell you how happy that makes me. I know that the car will be in the best person's hands, and I can retire peacefully."

Then, he said to me, "Now I want to do something for you!"

I looked at him with a puzzled look on my face and said, "What could you possibly do for me that you days end in time for supper or when the job is completed. When he can break away from his shop, his escape is to travel to Northern California and explore the solitude of the logging roads on his Kawasaki dirt bike.

After a lifetime of travel, his wife, Nanci, is no longer an enthusiastic traveler. For more than 50 years, she traveled with Bob to the *Hemi Under Glass* weekend events. She often had to fly back home on Sunday so that she could be at the school office on Monday morning. Now, she would rather do things centered around family and friends. Bob also eliminated the extensive traveling required to campaign the *Hemi Under Glass* from one event to another.

Bob has announced his last *Hemi Under Glass* wheels-up run multiple times, including 2017, 2018, and 2019. When asked if he would ever race the *Hemi Under Glass* again, Bob's response was, "All they have to do is ask me."

haven't already have done?"

He said to me, "I'm going to retire from driving, but I'm not going to retire from keeping busy. I'm going to help you restore the Grant Twin Engine Toronado. You know we have been talking about doing that car for years."

Truth be told, I had been begging Bob for years to help me restore the car! The table had turned, and now I was wiping tears from my eyes and couldn't talk for the second time in less than 24 hours. This was one of the happiest days of my life.

As this book is nearing completion in the summer of 2020, I've spoken about all this with coauthors Mark Fletcher and Rich Truesdell, whom I've come to know over the last few years. (Rich photographed myself, Bill, and Bob on the day in 2018 in Carlisle when the car passed to my custody. I say this as we don't own these cars; we are their caretakers). I'm proud to say that I've been that custodian of the car now for a couple of years, and here we are today with both the car in my garage and the damaged side of the car signed by none other than Jay Leno on my wall.

I had dear friend Rich Keylard airbrush portraits of Jay Leno and Bob Riggle to hang on the wall in my man cave/museum to commemorate that historic day. I proudly display the car and wall hanging in my collection of undoubtedly one of the best collections of Hurst vehicles on the planet.

The first thing that everyone asks when they come to my museum is, "Is that the car that rolled over with Jay Leno in the passenger seat?"

I love to tell people when they see my collection I couldn't think of a better certificate of authenticity than not only the car being restored but also the wall hanging above it.

Lou Hart

Over many years of attending US racing events, I have had the pleasure to meet and talk with Bob Riggle as well as be a spectator to his exhibition runs countless times in my younger days. Throughout the decades he has always been an approachable figure willing to sign autographs and share a few great stories of his racing moments. Cory Lee and I were fortunate to share some of those tales in the book we coauthored titled *Drag Racing's Exhibition Attractions: From Rockets to Ramp Jumps*.

One of my fondest memories of wheel-standers includes Bob Riggle and the *Hurst Hemi Under Glass*, as he was one of the original members of this special group, this fraternity. I witnessed the shower of sparks at night from the stands, amazed as the *Hurst Hemi Under Glass* disappeared down the track. Riggle was always a showman, and he made sure to give the fans a great show. Even so, the fans continually wanted more and returned multiple times to see his spectacular show.

Riggle has joyously entertained multiple generations, and I am proud to have participated in documenting a portion of his lengthy career.